The

Solitary Summer

by

Elizabeth von Arnim

Watchmaker Publishing
1905

ISBN 978-1-60386-326-1

To

The Man *of* Wrath

With

Some Apologies

&

Much Love

The House *from the* North End

May

May 2nd.–Last night after dinner, when we were in the garden, I said, "I want to be alone for a whole summer, and get to the very dregs of life. I want to be as idle as I can, so that my soul may have time to grow. Nobody shall be invited to stay with me, and if any one calls they will be told that I am out, or away, or sick. I shall spend the months in the garden, and on the plain, and in the forests. I shall watch the things that happen in my garden, and see where I have made mistakes. On wet days I will go into the thickest parts of the forests, where the pine needles are everlastingly dry, and when the sun shines I'll lie on the heath and see how the broom flares against the clouds. I shall be perpetually happy, because there will be no one to worry me. Out there on the plain there is silence, and where there is silence I have discovered there is peace."

"Mind you do not get your feet damp," said the Man of Wrath, removing his cigar.

It was the evening of May Day, and the spring had taken hold of me body and soul. The sky was full of stars, and the garden of scents, and the borders of wallflowers and sweet, sly pansies. All day there had been a breeze, and all day slow masses of white clouds had been sailing across the blue. Now it was so still, so motionless, so breathless, that it seemed as though a quiet hand had been laid on the garden, soothing and hushing it into silence.

The Man of Wrath sat at the foot of the verandah steps in that placid after-dinner mood which suffers fools, if not gladly, at least indulgently, and I stood in front of him, leaning against the sun-dial.

"Shall you take a book with you?" he asked.

"Yes, I shall," I replied, slightly nettled by his tone. "I am quite ready to admit that though the fields and flowers are always ready to teach, I am not always in the mood to learn, and sometimes my eyes are incapable of seeing things that at other times are quite plain."

"And then you read?"

"And then I read. Well, dear Sage, what of that?"

But he smoked in silence, and seemed suddenly absorbed by the stars.

"See," he said, after a pause, during which I stood looking at him and wishing he would use longer sentences, and he looked at the sky and did not think about me at all, "see how bright the stars are to-night. Almost as though it might freeze."

"It isn't going to freeze, and I won't look at anything until you have told me what you think of my idea. Wouldn't a whole lovely summer, quite alone, be delightful? Wouldn't it be perfect to get up every morning for weeks and feel that you belong to yourself and to nobody else?" And I went over to him and put a hand on each shoulder and gave him a little shake, for he persisted in gazing at the stars just as though I had not been there. "Please, Man of Wrath, say something long for once," I entreated; "you haven't said a good long sentence for a week."

He slowly brought his gaze from the stars down to me and smiled. Then he drew me on to his knee.

"Don't get affectionate," I urged; "it is words, not deeds, that I want. But I'll stay here if you'll talk."

"Well then, I will talk. What am I to say? You know you do as you please, and I never interfere with you. If you do not want to have any one here this summer you will not have any one, but you will find it a very long summer."

"No, I won't."

"And if you lie on the heath all day, people will think you are mad."

"What do I care what people think?"

"No, that is true. But you will catch cold, and your little nose will swell."

"Let it swell."

"And when it is hot you will be sunburnt and your skin spoilt."

"I don't mind my skin."

"And you will be dull."

"Dull?"

It often amuses me to reflect how very little the Man of Wrath really knows me. Here we have been three years buried in the country, and I as happy as a bird the whole time. I say as a bird, because other people have used the simile to describe absolute cheerfulness, although I do not believe birds are any happier than anyone else, and they quarrel disgracefully. I have been as happy then, we will say, as the best of birds, and have had seasons of solitude at intervals before now during which dull is the last word to describe my state of mind. Everybody, it is true, would not like it, and I had some visitors here a fortnight ago who left after staying about a week and clearly not enjoying themselves. They found it dull, I know, but that of course was their own fault; how can you make a person happy against his will? You can knock a great deal into him in the way of learning and what the schools call extras, but if you try for ever you will not knock any happiness into a being who has not got it in him to be happy. The only result probably would be that you knock your own out of yourself. Obviously happiness must come from within, and not from without; and judging from my past experience and my present sensations, I should say that I have a store just now within me more than sufficient to fill five quiet months.

"I wonder," I remarked after a pause, during which I began to suspect that I too must belong to the serried ranks of the *femmes incomprises*, "why you think I shall be dull. The garden is always beautiful, and I am nearly always in the mood to enjoy it. Not quite always, I must confess, for when those Schmidts were here" (their name was not Schmidt, but what does that matter?) "I grew almost to hate it. Whenever I went into it there they were, dragging themselves about with faces full of indignant resignation. Do you suppose they saw one of those blue hepaticas overflowing the shrubberies? And when I drove with them into the woods, where the fairies were so busy just then hanging the branches with little green jewels, they talked about Berlin the whole time, and the good savouries their new chef makes."

"Well, my dear, no doubt they missed their savouries. Your garden, I acknowledge, is growing very pretty, but your cook is bad. Poor Schmidt sometimes looked quite ill at dinner, and the beauty of your floral arrangements in no way made up for the inferior quality of the food. Send her away."

"Send her away? Be thankful you have her. A bad cook is more effectual a great deal than Kissingen and Carlsbad and Homburg rolled into one, and very much cheaper. As long as I have her, my dear man, you will be comparatively thin and amiable. Poor Schmidt, as you call him, eats too much of those delectable savouries, and then looks at his wife and wonders why he married her. Don't let me catch you doing that."

"I do not think it is very likely," said the Man of Wrath; but whether he meant it prettily, or whether he was merely thinking of the improbability of his ever eating too much of the local savouries, I cannot tell. I object, however, to discussing cooks in the garden on a starlight night, so I got off his knee and proposed that we should stroll round a little.

It was such a sweet evening, such a fitting close to a beautiful May Day, and the flowers shone in the twilight like pale stars, and the air was full of fragrance, and I envied the bats fluttering through such a bath of scent, with the real stars above and the pansy stars beneath, and themselves so fashioned that even if they wanted to they could not make a noise and disturb the prevailing peace. A great deal that is poetical has been written by English people about May Day, and the impression left on the foreign mind is an impression of posies, and garlands, and village greens, and youths and maidens much be-ribboned, and lambs, and general friskiness. I was in England once on a May Day, and we sat over the fire shivering and listening blankly to the north- east wind tearing down the street and the rattling of the hail against the windows, and the friends with whom I was staying said it was very often so, and that they had never seen any lambs and ribbons. We Germans attach no poetical significance to it at all, and yet we well might, for it is almost invariably beautiful; and as for garlands, I wonder how many villages full of young people could have been provided with them out of my garden, and nothing be missed. It is to-day a garden of wallflowers, and I think I have every colour and sort in cultivation. The borders under the south windows of the house, so empty and melancholy this time last year, are crammed with them, and are finished off in front by a broad strip from end to end of yellow and white pansies. The tea rose beds round the sun-dial facing these borders are sheets of white, and golden, and purple, and wine-red pansies, with the dainty red shoots of the tea roses presiding delicately in their midst. The verandah steps leading down into this pansy paradise have boxes of white, and pink, and yellow tulips all the way up on each side, and on the lawn, behind the roses, are two big beds of every coloured tulip rising above a carpet of forget-me-nots. How very much more charming different-coloured tulips are together than tulips in one colour by itself! Last year, on the recommendation of sundry writers about gardens, I tried beds of scarlet tulips and forget-me-nots. They were pretty enough; but I wish those writers could see my beds of mixed tulips. I never saw anything so sweetly, delicately gay. The only ones I exclude are the rose-coloured ones; but scarlet, gold, delicate pink, and white are all there, and the effect is infinitely enchanting. The forget-me-nots grow taller as the tulips go off, and will presently tenderly engulf them altogether, and so hide the shame of their decay in their kindly little arms. They will be left there, clouds of gentle blue, until the tulips are well withered, and then they will be taken away to make room for the scarlet geraniums that are to occupy these two beds in the summer and flare in the sun as much as they like. I love an occasional mass of fiery colour, and these two will make the lilies look even whiter and more breathless that are to stand sentinel round the semicircle containing the precious tea roses.

The first two years I had this garden, I was determined to do exactly as I chose in it, and to have no arrangements of plants that I had not planned, and no plants but those I knew and loved; so, fearing that an experienced gardener would profit by my ignorance, then about as absolute as it could be, and thrust all his bedding nightmares upon me, and fill the place with those dreadful salad arrangements so often seen in the gardens of the indifferent rich, I would only have a meek man of small pretensions, who would be easily persuaded that I knew as much as, or more than, he did himself. I had three of these meek men one after the other, and learned what I might long ago have discovered, that the less a person knows, the more certain he is that he is right, and that no weapons yet invented are of any use in a struggle with stupidity. The first of these three went melancholy mad at the end of a year; the second was love-sick, and threw down his tools and gave up his situation to wander after the departed siren who had turned his head; the third, when I inquired how it was that the things he had sown never by any chance came up, scratched his head, and as this is a sure sign of ineptitude, I sent him away.

Then I sat down and thought. I had been here two years and worked hard, through these men, at the garden; I had done my best to learn all I could and make it beautiful; I had refused to have more than an inferior gardener because of his supposed more perfect obedience, and one assistant, because of my desire to enjoy the garden undisturbed; I had studied diligently all the gardening books I could lay hands on; I was under the impression that I am an ordinarily intelligent person, and that if an ordinarily intelligent person devotes his whole time to studying a subject he loves, success is very probable; and yet at the end of two years what was my garden like? The failures of the first two summers had been regarded with philosophy; but that third summer I used to go into it sometimes and cry.

As far as I was concerned I had really learned a little, and knew what to buy, and had fairly correct notions as to when and in what soil to sow and plant what I had bought; but of what use is it to buy good seeds and plants and bulbs if you are forced to hand them over to a gardener who listens with ill-concealed impatience to the careful directions you give him, says Jawohl a great many times, and then goes off and puts them in the way he has always done, which is invariably the wrong way? My hands were tied because of the unfortunate circumstance of sex, or I would gladly have changed places with him and requested him to do the talking while I did the planting, and as he probably would not have talked much there would have been a distinct gain in the peace of the world, which would surely be very materially increased if women's tongues were tied instead of their hands, and those that want to could work with them without collecting a crowd. And is it not certain that the more one's body works the fainter grow the waggings of one's tongue? I sometimes literally ache with envy as I watch the men going about their pleasant work in the sunshine, turning up the luscious damp earth, raking, weeding, watering, planting, cutting the grass, pruning the trees—not a thing that they do from the first uncovering of the roses in the spring to the November bonfires but fills my soul with longing to be up and doing it too. A great many things will have to happen, however, before such a state of popular large-mindedness as will allow of my digging without creating a sensation is reached, so I have plenty of time for further grumblings; only I do very much wish that the tongues inhabiting this apparently lonely and deserted countryside would restrict their comments to the sins, if any, committed by the indigenous females (since sins are fair game for comment) and leave their harmless eccentricities alone. After having driven through vast tracts of forest and heath for hours, and never meeting a soul or seeing a house, it is surprising to be told that on such a day you took such a drive and were at such a spot; yet this has happened to me more than once. And if even this is watched and noted, with what lightning rapidity would the news spread that I had been seen stalking down the garden path with a hoe over my shoulder and a basket in my hand, and weeding written large on every feature! Yet I should love to weed.

I think it was the way the weeds flourished that put an end at last to my hesitations about taking an experienced gardener and giving him a reasonable number of helpers, for I found that much as I enjoyed privacy, I yet detested nettles more, and the nettles appeared really to pick out those places to grow in where my sweetest things were planted, and utterly defied the three meek men when they made periodical and feeble efforts to get rid of them. I have a large heart in regard to things that grow, and many a weed that would not be tolerated anywhere else is allowed to live and multiply undisturbed in my garden. They are such pretty things, some of them, such charmingly audacious things, and it is so particularly nice of them to do all their growing, and flowering, and seed-bearing without any help or any encouragement. I admit I feel vexed if they are so officious as to push up among my tea roses and pansies, and I also prefer my paths without them; but on the grass, for instance, why not let the poor little creatures enjoy themselves quietly, instead of going out with a dreadful instrument and viciously digging them up one by one? Once I went into the garden just as the last of the three inept ones had taken up his stand, armed with this implement, in the middle of the sheet of gold and silver that is known for convenience' sake as the lawn, and was scratching his head, as he looked round, in a futile effort to decide where he should begin. I saved the dandelions and daisies on that occasion, and I like to believe they know it. They certainly look very jolly when I come out, and I rather fancy the dandelions dig each other in their little ribs when they see me, and whisper, "Here comes Elizabeth; she's a good sort, ain't she?"–for of course dandelions do not express themselves very elegantly.

But nettles are not to be tolerated. They settled the question on which I had been turning my back for so long, and one fine August morning, when there seemed to be nothing in the garden but nettles, and it was hard to believe that we had ever been doing anything but carefully cultivating them in all their varieties, I walked into the Man of Wrath's den.

"My dear man," I began, in the small caressing voice of one who has long been obstinate and is in the act of giving in, "will you kindly advertise for a head gardener and a proper number of assistants? Nearly all the bulbs and seeds and plants I have squandered my money and my hopes on have turned out to be nettles, and I don't like them. I have had a wretched summer, and never want to see a meek gardener again."

"My dear Elizabeth," he replied, "I regret that you did not take my advice sooner. How often have I pointed out the folly of engaging one incapable person after the other? The vegetables, when we get any, are uneatable, and there is never any fruit. I do not in the least doubt your good intentions, but you are wanting in judgment. When will you learn to rely on my experience?"

I hung my head; for was he not in the pleasant position of being able to say, "I told you so"?–which indeed he has been saying for the last two years. "I don't like relying," I murmured, "and have rather a prejudice against somebody else's experience. Please will you send the advertisement to-day?"

They came in such shoals that half the population must have been head gardeners out of situations. I took all the likely ones round the garden, and I do not think I ever spent a more chastening week than that week of selection. Their remarks were, naturally, of the frankest nature, as I had told them I had had practically only gardeners' assistants since I lived here, and they had no idea, when they were politely scoffing at some arrangement, that it happened to be one of my own. The hot-beds in the kitchen garden with which I had taken such pains were objects of special derision. It appeared that they were all wrong–measurements, preparation, soil, manure, everything that could be wrong, was. Certainly the only crop we had from them was weeds. But I began about half way through the week to grow sceptical, because on comparing their criticisms I found they seldom agreed, and so took courage again. Finally I chose a nice, trim young man, with strikingly intelligent eyes and quick movements, who had shown himself less concerned with the state of chaos existing than with considerations of what might eventually be made of the place. He is very deaf, so he wastes no time in words, and is exceedingly keen on gardening, and knows, as I very soon discovered, a vast amount more than I do, in spite of my three years' application. Moreover, he is filled with that humility and eagerness to learn which is only found in those who have already learned more than their neighbours. He enters into my plans with enthusiasm, and makes suggestions of his own, which, if not always quite in accordance with what are perhaps my peculiar tastes, at least plainly show that he understands his business. We had a very busy winter together altering all the beds, for they none of them had been given a soil in which plants could grow, and next autumn I intend to have all the so-called lawns dug up and levelled, and shall see whether I cannot have decent turf here. I told him he must save the daisy and dandelion roots, and he looked rather crestfallen at that, but he is young, and can learn to like what I like, and get rid of his only fault, a nursery- gardener attitude towards all flowers that are not the fashion. "I shall want a great many daffodils next spring," I shouted one day at the beginning of our acquaintance.

His eyes gleamed. "Ah yes," he said with immediate approval, "they are *sehr modern*."

I was divided between amusement at the notion of Spenser's daffadowndillies being *modern*, and indignation at hearing exactly the same adjective applied to them that the woman who sells me my hats bestows on the most appalling examples of her stock.

"They are to be in troops on the grass," I said; whereupon his face grew doubtful. "That is indeed *sehr modern*," I shouted. But he had grown suddenly deafer—a phenomenon I have observed to occur every time my orders are such as he has never been given before. After a time he will, I think, become imbued with my unorthodoxy in these matters; and meanwhile he has the true gardening spirit and loves his work, and love, after all, is the chief thing. I know of no compost so good. In the poorest soil, love alone, by itself, will work wonders.

Down the garden path, past the copse of lilacs with their swelling dark buds, and the great three-cornered bed of tea roses and pansies in front of it, between the rows of china roses and past the lily and foxglove groups, we came last night to the spring garden in the open glade round the old oak; and there, the first to flower of the flowering trees, and standing out like a lovely white naked thing against the dusk of the evening, was a double cherry in full bloom, while close beside it, but not so visible so late, with all their graceful growth outlined by rosy buds, were two Japanese crab apples. The grass just there is filled with narcissus, and at the foot of the oak a colony of tulips consoles me for the loss of the purple crocus patches, so lovely a little while since.

"I must be by myself for once a whole summer through," I repeated, looking round at these things with a feeling of hardly being able to bear their beauty, and the beauty of the starry sky, and the beauty of the silence and the scent—"I must be alone, so that I shall not miss one of these wonders, and have leisure really to *live*."

"Very well, my dear," replied the Man of Wrath, "only do not grumble afterwards when you find it dull. You shall be solitary if you choose, and, as far as I am concerned, I will invite no one. It is always best to allow a woman to do as she likes if you can, and it saves a good deal of bother. To have what she desired is generally an effective punishment."

"Dear Sage," I cried, slipping my hand through his arm, "don't be so wise! I promise you that I won't be dull, and I won't be punished, and I will be happy."

And we sauntered slowly back to the house in great contentment, discussing the firmament and such high things, as though we knew all about them.

May 15th.—There is a dip in the rye-fields about half a mile from my garden gate, a little round hollow like a dimple, with water and reeds at the bottom, and a few water-loving trees and bushes on the shelving ground around. Here I have been nearly every morning lately, for it suits the mood I am in, and I like the narrow footpath to it through the rye, and I like its solitary dampness in a place where everything is parched, and when I am lying on the grass and look down I can see the reeds glistening greenly in the water, and when I look up I can see the rye-fringe brushing the sky. All sorts of beasts come and stare at me, and larks sing above me, and creeping things crawl over me, and stir in the long grass beside me; and here I bring my book, and read and dream away the profitable morning hours, to the accompaniment of the amorous croakings of innumerable frogs.

Thoreau has been my companion for some days past, it having struck me as more appropriate to bring him out to a pond than to read him, as was hitherto my habit, on Sunday mornings in the garden. He is a person who loves the open air, and will refuse to give you much pleasure if you try to read him

amid the pomp and circumstance of upholstery; but out in the
sun, and especially by this pond, he is delightful, and we spend
the happiest hours together, he making statements, and I either
agreeing heartily, or just laughing and reserving my opinion till I
shall have more ripely considered the thing. He, of course, does
not like me as much as I like him, because I live in a cloud of
dust and germs produced by wilful superfluity of furniture, and
have not the courage to get a match and set light to it: and every
day he sees the door-mat on which I wipe my shoes on going
into the house, in defiance of his having told me that he had
once refused the offer of one on the ground that it is best to
avoid even the beginnings of evil. But my philosophy has not yet
reached the acute stage that will enable me to see a door-mat in
its true character as a hinderer of the development of souls, and
I like to wipe my shoes. Perhaps if I had to live with few
servants, or if it were possible, short of existence in a cave, to do
without them altogether, I should also do without door-mats,
and probably in summer without shoes too, and wipe my feet on
the grass nature no doubt provides for this purpose; and
meanwhile we know that though he went to the woods, Thoreau
came back again, and lived for the rest of his days like other
people. During his life, I imagine he would have refused to
notice anything so fatiguing as an ordinary German woman, and
never would have deigned discourse to me on the themes he
loved best; but now his spirit belongs to me, and all he thought,
and believed, and felt, and he talks as much and as intimately to
me here in my solitude as ever he did to his dearest friends years
ago in Concord. In the garden he was a pleasant companion, but
in the lonely dimple he is fascinating, and the morning hours
hurry past at a quite surprising rate when he is with me, and it
grieves me to be obliged to interrupt him in the middle of some
quaint sentence or beautiful thought just because the sun is
touching a certain bush down by the water's edge, which is a sign
that it is lunch-time and that I must be off. Back we go together
through the rye, he carefully tucked under one arm, while with
the other I brandish a bunch of grass to keep off the flies that
appear directly we emerge into the sunshine. "Oh, my dear
Thoreau," I murmur sometimes, overcome by the fierce heat of

the little path at noonday and the persistence of the flies, "did you have flies at Walden to exasperate you? And what became of your philosophy then?" But he never notices my plaints, and I know that inside his covers he is discoursing away like anything on the folly of allowing oneself to be overwhelmed in that terrible rapid and whirlpool called a dinner, which is situated in the meridian shallows, and of the necessity, if one would keep happy, of sailing by it looking another way, tied to the mast like Ulysses. But he gets grimly carried back for all that, and is taken into the house and put on his shelf and left there, because I still happen to have a body attached to my spirit, which, if not fed at the ordinary time, becomes a nuisance. Yet he is right; luncheon is a snare of the tempter, and I would perhaps try to sail by it like Ulysses if I had a biscuit in my pocket to comfort me, but there are the babies to be fed, and the Man of Wrath, and how can a respectable wife and mother sail past any meridian shallows in which those dearest to her have stuck? So I stand by them, and am punished every day by that two-o'clock-in-the-afternoon feeling to which I so much object, and yet cannot avoid. It is mortifying, after the sunshiny morning hours at my pond, when I feel as though I were almost a poet, and very nearly a philosopher, and wholly a joyous animal in an ecstasy of love with life, to come back and live through those dreary luncheon-ridden hours, when the soul is crushed out of sight and sense by cutlets and asparagus and revengeful sweet things. My morning friend turns his back on me when I reenter the library; nor do I ever touch him in the afternoon. Books have their idiosyncrasies as well as people, and will not show me their full beauties unless the place and time in which they are read suits them. If, for instance, I cannot read Thoreau in a drawing-room, how much less would I ever dream of reading Boswell in the grass by a pond! Imagine carrying him off in company with his great friend to a lonely dell in a rye-field, and expecting them to be entertaining. "Nay, my dear lady," the great man would say in mighty tones of rebuke, "this will never do. Lie in a rye-field? What folly is that? And who would converse in a damp hollow that can help it?" So I read and laugh over my Boswell in the library when the lamps are lit, buried in cushions and surrounded by every sign of civilisation, with the drawn curtains shutting out the garden and the country solitude so much disliked by both sage and disciple. Indeed, it is Bozzy who asserts that in the country the only things that make one happy are meals. "I was happy," he says, when stranded at a place called Corrichatachin in the Island of Skye, and unable to get out of it because of the rain,–"I was happy when tea came. Such I take it is the state of those who live in the country. Meals are wished for from the cravings of vacuity of mind, as well as from the desire of eating." And such is the perverseness of human nature that Boswell's wisdom delights me even more than Johnson's, though I love them both very heartily.

In the afternoon I potter in the garden with Goethe. He did not, I am sure, care much really about flowers and gardens, yet he said many lovely things about them that remain in one's memory just as persistently as though they had been inspired expressions of actual feelings; and the intellect must indeed have been gigantic that could so beautifully pretend. Ordinary blunderers have to feel a vast amount before they can painfully stammer out a sentence that will describe it; and when they have got it out, how it seems to have just missed the core of the sensation that gave it birth, and what a poor, weak child it is of what was perhaps a mighty feeling! I read Goethe on a special seat, never departed from when he accompanies me, a seat on the south side of an ice-house, and thus sheltered from the north winds sometimes prevalent in May, and shaded by the low-hanging branches of a great beech-tree from more than flickering sunshine. Through these branches I can see a group of giant poppies just coming into flower, flaming out beyond the trees on the grass, and farther down a huge silver birch, its first spring green not yet deepened out of delicacy, and looking almost golden backed by a solemn cluster of firs. Here I read Goethe– everything I have of his, both what is well known and what is not; here I shed invariable tears over Werther, however often I read it; here I wade through Wilhelm Meister, and sit in amazement before the complications of the Wahlverwandschaften; here I am plunged in wonder and wretchedness by Faust; and here I sometimes walk up and down in the shade and apostrophise the tall firs at the bottom of the glade in the opening soliloquy of Iphigenia. Every now and then I leave the book on the seat and go and have a refreshing potter among my flower beds, from which I return greatly benefited, and with a more just conception of what, in this world, is worth bothering about, and what is not.

In the evening, when everything is tired and quiet, I sit with Walt Whitman by the rose beds and listen to what that lonely and beautiful spirit has to tell me of night, sleep, death, and the stars. This dusky, silent hour is his; and this is the time when I can best hear the beatings of that most tender and generous heart. Such great love, such rapture of jubilant love for nature, and the good green grass, and trees, and clouds, and sunlight; such aching anguish of love for all that breathes and is sick and sorry; such passionate longing to help and mend and comfort that which never can be helped and mended and comforted; such eager looking to death, delicate death, as the one complete and final consolation–before this revelation of yearning, universal pity, every-day selfishness stands awe-struck and ashamed.

When I drive in the forests, Keats goes with me; and if I extend my drive to the Baltic shores, and spend the afternoon on the moss beneath the pines whose pink stems form the framework of the sea, I take Spenser; and presently the blue waves are the ripples of the Idle Lake, and a tiny white sail in the distance is Phaedria's shallow ship, bearing Cymochles swiftly away to her drowsy little nest of delights. How can I tell why Keats has never been brought here, and why Spenser is brought again and again? Who shall follow the dark intricacies of the elementary female mind? It is safer not to attempt to do so, but by simply cataloguing them collectively under the heading Instinct, have done with them once and for all.

What a blessing it is to love books. Everybody must love something, and I know of no objects of love that give such substantial and unfailing returns as books and a garden. And how easy it would have been to come into the world without this, and possessed instead of an all-consuming passion, say, for hats, perpetually raging round my empty soul! I feel I owe my forefathers a debt of gratitude, for I suppose the explanation is that they too did not care for hats. In the centre of my library there is a wooden pillar propping up the ceiling, and preventing it, so I am told, from tumbling about our ears; and round this pillar, from floor to ceiling, I have had shelves fixed, and on these shelves are all the books that I have read again and again, and hope to read many times more—all the books, that is, that I love quite the best. In the bookcases round the walls are many that I love, but here in the centre of the room, and easiest to get at, are those I love the *best*—the very elect among my favourites. They change from time to time as I get older, and with years some that are in the bookcases come here, and some that are here go into the bookcases, and some again are removed altogether, and are placed on certain shelves in the drawing-room which are reserved for those that have been weighed in the balance and found wanting, and from whence they seldom, if ever, return. Carlyle used to be among the elect. That was years ago, when my hair was very long, and my skirts very short, and I sat in the paternal groves with *Sartor Resartus*, and felt full of wisdom and *Weltschmerz*; and even after I was married, when we lived in town, and the noise of his thunderings was almost drowned by the rattle of droschkies over the stones in the street below, he still shone forth a bright, particular star. Now, whether it is age creeping upon me, or whether it is that the country is very still and sound carries, or whether my ears have grown sensitive, I know not; but the moment I open him there rushes out such a clatter of denunciation, and vehemence, and wrath, that I am completely deafened; and as I easily get bewildered, and love peace, and my chief aim is to follow the apostle's advice and study to be quiet, he has been degraded from his high position round the pillar and has gone into retirement against the wall, where the accident of alphabet causes him to rest in the soothing society of one Carina, a harmless gentleman, whose book on the *Bagni di Lucca* is on his left, and a Frenchman of the name of Charlemagne, whose soporific comedy written at the beginning of the century and called *Le Testament de l'Oncle, ou Les Lunettes Cassees*, is next to him on his right. Two works of his still remain, however, among the elect, though differing in glory—his

Frederick the Great, fascinating for obvious reasons to the patriotic German mind, and his *Life of Sterling*, a quiet book on the whole, a record of an uneventful life, in which the natural positions of subject and biographer are reversed, the man of genius writing the life of the unimportant friend, and the fact that the friend was exceedingly lovable in no way lessening one's discomfort in the face of such an anomaly. Carlyle stands on an eminence altogether removed from Sterling, who stands, indeed, on no eminence at all, unless it be an eminence, that (happily) crowded bit of ground, where the bright and courageous and lovable stand together. We Germans have all heard of Carlyle, and many of us have read him with due amazement, our admiration often interrupted by groans at the difficulties his style places in the candid foreigner's path; but without Carlyle which of us would ever have heard of Sterling? And even in this comparatively placid book mines of the accustomed vehemence are sprung on the shrinking reader. To the prosaic German, nourished on a literature free from thunderings and any marked acuteness of enthusiasm, Carlyle is an altogether astonishing phenomenon.

And here I feel constrained to inquire sternly who I am that I should talk in this unbecoming manner of Carlyle? To which I reply that I am only a humble German seeking after peace, devoid of the least real desire to criticise anybody, and merely anxious to get out of the way of geniuses when they make too much noise. All I want is to read quietly the books that I at present prefer. Carlyle is shut up now and therefore silent on his comfortable shelf; yet who knows but what in my old age, when I begin to feel really young, I may not once again find comfort in him?

What a medley of books there is round my pillar! Here is Jane Austen leaning against Heine–what would she have said to that, I wonder?–with Miss Mitford and *Cranford* to keep her in countenance on her other side. Here is my Goethe, one of many editions I have of him, the one that has made the acquaintance of the ice-house and the poppies. Here are Ruskin, Lubbock, White's *Selborne*, Izaak Walton, Drummond, Herbert Spencer (only as much of him as I hope I understand and am afraid I do not), Walter Pater, Matthew Arnold, Thoreau, Lewis Carroll,

Oliver Wendell Holmes, Hawthorne, *Wuthering Heights, Lamb's Essays, Johnson's Lives*, Marcus Aurelius, Montaigne, Gibbon, the immortal Pepys, the egregious Boswell, various American children's books that I loved as a child and read and love to this day; various French children's books, loved for the same reason; whole rows of German children's books, on which I was brought up, with their charming woodcuts of quaint little children in laced bodices, and good housemothers cutting bread and butter, and descriptions of the atmosphere of fearful innocence and pure religion and swift judgments and rewards in which they lived, and how the *Finger Gottes* was impressed on everything that happened to them; all the poets; most of the dramatists; and, I verily believe, every gardening book and book about gardens that has been published of late years.

These gardening books are an unfailing delight, especially in winter, when to sit by my blazing peat fire with the snow driving past the windows and read the luscious descriptions of roses and all the other summer glories is one of my greatest pleasures. And then how well I get to know and love those gardens whose gradual development has been described by their owners, and how happily I wander in fancy down the paths of certain specially charming ones in Lancashire, Berkshire, Surrey, and Kent, and admire the beautiful arrangement of bed and border, and the charming bits in unexpected corners, and all the evidences of untiring love! Any book I see advertised that treats of gardens I immediately buy, and thus possess quite a collection of fascinating and instructive garden literature. A few are feeble, and get shunted off into the drawing-room; but the others stay with me winter and summer, and soon lose the gloss of their new coats, and put on the comfortable look of old friends in every-day clothes, under the frequent touch of affection. They are such special friends that I can hardly pass them without a nod and a smile at the well-known covers, each of which has some pleasant association of time and place to make it still more dear.

My spirit too has wandered in one or two French gardens, but has not yet heard of a German one loved beyond everything by its owner. It is, of course, possible that my countrymen do love them and keep quiet about them, but many things are possible that are not probable, and experience compels me to the opinion that this is one of them. We have the usual rich man who has fine gardens laid out regardless of expense, but those are not gardens in the sense I mean; and we have the poor man with his bit of ground, hardly ever treated otherwise than as a fowl-run or a place dedicated to potatoes; and as for the middle class, it is too busy hurrying through life to have time or inclination to stop and plant a rose.

How glad I am I need not hurry. What a waste of life, just getting and spending. Sitting by my pansy beds, with the slow clouds floating leisurely past, and all the clear day before me, I look on at the hot scramble for the pennies of existence and am lost in wonder at the vulgarity that pushes, and cringes, and tramples, untiring and unabashed. And when you have got your pennies, what then? They are only pennies, after all–unpleasant, battered copper things, without a gold piece among them, and never worth the degradation of self, and the hatred of those below you who have fewer, and the derision of those above you who have more. And as I perceive I am growing wise, and what is even worse, allegorical, and as these are tendencies to be fought against as long as possible, I'll go into the garden and play with the babies, who at this moment are sitting in a row on the buttercups, singing what appear to be selections from popular airs.

The Library

June

June 3rd.–The Man of Wrath, I observe, is laying traps for me and being deep. He has prophesied that I will find solitude intolerable, and he is naturally desirous that his prophecy should be fulfilled. He knows that continuous rain depresses me, and he is awaiting a spell of it to bring me to a confession that I was wrong after all, whereupon he will make that remark so precious to the married heart, "My dear, I told you so." He begins the day by tapping the barometer, looking at the sky, and shaking his head. If there are any clouds he remarks that they are coming up, and if there are none he says it is too fine to last. He has even gone the length once or twice of starting off to the farm on hot, sunny mornings in his mackintosh, in order to impress on me beyond all doubt that the weather is breaking up. He studiously keeps out of my way all day, so that I may have every opportunity of being bored as quickly as possible, and in the evenings he retires to his den directly after dinner, muttering something about letters. When he has finally disappeared, I go out to the stars and laugh at his transparent wiles.

But how would it be if we did have a spell of wet weather? I do not quite know. As long as it is fine, rainy days in the future do not seem so very terrible, and one, or even two really wet ones are quite enjoyable when they do come–pleasant times that remind one of the snug winter now so far off, times of reading, and writing, and paying one's bills. I never pay bills or write letters on fine summer days. Not for any one will I forego all that such a day rightly spent out of doors might give me; so that a wet day at intervals is almost as necessary for me as for my garden. But how would it be if there were many wet days? I believe a week of steady drizzle in summer is enough to make the stoutest heart depressed. It is to be borne in winter by the simple expedient of turning your face to the fire; but when you have no fire, and very long days, your cheerfulness slowly slips away, and the dreariness prevailing out of doors comes in and broods in the blank corners of your heart. I rather fancy, however, that it is a waste of energy to ponder over what I should do if we had a wet summer on such a radiant day as this. I prefer sitting here on the verandah and looking down through a frame of leaves at all the rosebuds June has put in the beds round the sun-dial, to ponder over nothing, and just be glad that I am alive. The verandah at two o'clock on a summer's afternoon is a place in which to be happy and not decide anything, as my friend Thoreau told me of some other tranquil spot this morning. The chairs are comfortable, there is a table to write on, and the shadows of young leaves flicker across the paper. On one side a Crimson Rambler is thrusting inquisitive shoots through the wooden bars, being able this year for the first time since it was planted to see what I am doing up here, and next to it a Jackmanni clematis clings with soft young fingers to anything it thinks likely to help it up to the goal of its ambition, the roof. I wonder which of the two will get there first. Down there in the rose beds, among the hundreds of buds there is only one full-blown rose as yet, a Marie van Houtte, one of the loveliest of the tea roses, perfect in shape and scent and colour, and in my garden always the first rose to flower; and the first flowers it bears are the loveliest of its own lovely flowers, as though it felt that the first of its children to see the sky and the sun and the familiar garden after the winter sleep ought to put on the very daintiest clothes they can muster for such a festal occasion.

Through the open schoolroom windows I can hear the two eldest babies at their lessons. The village schoolmaster comes over every afternoon and teaches them for two hours, so that we are free from governesses in the house, and once those two hours are over they are free for twenty-four from anything in the shape of learning. The schoolroom is next to the verandah, and as two o'clock approaches their excitement becomes more and more intense, and they flutter up and down the steps, looking in their white dresses like angels on a Jacob's ladder, or watch eagerly among the bushes for a first glimpse of him, like miniature and perfectly proper Isoldes. He is a kind giant with that endless supply of patience so often found in giants, especially when they happen to be village schoolmasters, and judging from the amount of laughter I hear, the babies seem to enjoy their lessons in a way they never did before. Every day they prepare bouquets for him, and he gets more of them than a *prima donna*, or at any rate a more regular supply. The first day he came I was afraid they would be very shy of such a big strange man, and that he would extract nothing from them but tears; but the moment I left them alone together and as I shut the door, I heard them eagerly informing him, by way of opening the friendship, that their heads were washed every Saturday night, and that their hair-ribbons did not match because there had not been enough of the one sort to go round. I went away hoping that they would not think it necessary to tell him how often my head is washed, or any other news of a personal nature about me; but I believe by this time that man knows everything there is to know about the details of my morning toilet, which is daily watched with the greatest interest by the Three. I hope he will be more successful than I was in teaching them Bible stories. I never got farther than Noah, at which stage their questions became so searching as to completely confound me; and as no one likes being confounded, and it is especially regrettable when a parent is placed in such a position, I brought the course to an abrupt end by assuming that owl-like air of wisdom peculiar to infallibility in a corner, and telling them that they were too young to understand these things for the present; and they, having a touching faith in the truth of every word I say, gave three contented little purrs of assent, and proposed that we should play instead at rolling down the grass bank under the south windows–which I did not do, I am glad to remember.

But the schoolmaster, after four weeks' teaching, has got them as far as Moses, and safely past the Noah's ark on which I came to grief, and if glibness is a sign of knowledge then they have learned the story very thoroughly. Yesterday, after he had gone, they emerged into the verandah fresh from Moses and bursting with eagerness to tell me all about it.

"Herr Schenk told us to-day about Moses," began the April baby, making a rush at me.

"Oh?"

"Yes, and a *boser, boser Konig* who said every boy must be deaded, and Moses was the *allerliebster.*"

"Talk English, my *dear* baby, and not such a dreadful mixture," I besought.

"He wasn't a cat."

"A cat?"

"Yes, he wasn't a cat, that Moses—a boy was he."

"But of course he wasn't a cat," I said with some severity; "no one ever supposed he was."

"Yes, but mummy," she explained eagerly, with much appropriate hand- action, "the cook's Moses *is* a cat."

"Oh, I see. Well?"

"And he was put in a basket in the water, and that did swim. And then one time they comed, and she said—"

"Who came? And who said?"

"Why, the ladies; and the *Konigstochter* said, *'Ach hormal, da schreit so etwas.'*"

"In German?"

"Yes, and then they went near, and one must take off her shoes and stockings and go in the water and fetch that tiny basket, and then they made it open, and that *Kind* did cry and cry and *strampel* so"—here both the babies gave such a vivid illustration of the *strampeln* that the verandah shook—"and see! it is a tiny baby. And they fetched somebody to give it to eat, and the *Konigstochter* can keep that boy, and further it doesn't go."

"Do you love Moses, mummy?" asked the May baby, jumping into my lap, and taking my face in both her hands—one of the many pretty, caressing little ways of a very pretty, caressing little creature.

"Yes," I replied bravely, "I love him."

"Then I too!" they cried with simultaneous gladness, the seal having thus been affixed to the legitimacy of their regard for him. To be of such authority that your verdict on every subject under heaven is absolute and final is without doubt to be in a proud position, but, like all proud positions, it bristles with pitfalls and drawbacks to the weak-kneed; and most of my conversations with the babies end in a sudden change of subject made necessary by the tendency of their remarks and the unanswerableness of their arguments. Happily, yesterday the Moses talk was brought to an end by the April baby herself, who suddenly remembered that I had not yet seen and sympathised with her dearest possession, a Dutch doll called Mary Jane, since a lamentable accident had bereft it of both its legs; and she had dived into the schoolroom and fished it out of the dark corner reserved for the mangled and thrust it in my face before I had well done musing on the nature and extent of my love for Moses—for I try to be conscientious—and bracing myself to meet the next question.

"See this poor Mary Jane," she said, her voice and hand quivering with tenderness as she lifted its petticoats to show me the full extent of the calamity, "see, mummy, no legs—only twowsers and nothing further."

I wish they would speak English a little better. The pains I take to correct them and weed out the German words that crop up in every sentence are really untiring, and the results discouraging. Indeed, as they get older the German asserts itself more and more, and is threatening to swallow up the little English they have left entirely. I talk English steadily with them, but everybody else, including a small French nurse lately imported, nothing but German. Somebody told me the thing to do was to let children pick up languages when they were babies, at which period they absorb them as easily as food and drink, and are quite unaware that they are learning anything at all; whereupon I immediately introduced this French girl into the family, forgetting how little English they have absorbed, and the result has been that they pass their days delightfully in teaching her German. They were astonished at first on discovering that she could not understand a word they said, and soon set about altering such an uncomfortable state of things; and as they are three to one and very zealous, and she is a meek little person with a profile like a teapot with a twisted black handle of hair, their success was practically certain from the beginning, and she is getting on quite nicely with her German, and has at least already thoroughly learned all the mistakes. She wanders in the garden with a surprised look on her face as of one who is moving about in worlds not realised; and the three cling to her skirts and give her enthusiastic lessons all day long.

Poor Seraphine! What courage to weigh anchor at eighteen and go into a foreign country, to a place where you are among utter strangers, without a friend, unable to speak a word of the language, and not even sure before you start whether you will be given enough to eat. Either it is that saddest of courage forced on the timid by necessity, or, as Doctor Johnson would probably have said, it is stark insensibility; and I am afraid when I look at her I silently agree with the apostle of common sense, and take it for granted that she is incapable of deep feeling, for the altogether inadequate reason that she has a certain resemblance to a teapot. Now is it not hard that a person may have a soul as beautiful as an angel's, a dwelling-place for all sweet sounds and harmonies, and if nature has not thought fit to endow his body with a chin the world will have none of him? The vulgar prejudice is in favour of chins, and who shall escape its influence? I, for one, cannot, though theoretically I utterly reject the belief that the body is the likeness of the soul; for has not each of us friends who, we know, love beyond everything that which is noble and good, and who by no means themselves look noble and good? And what about all the beautiful persons who love nothing on earth except themselves? Yet who in the world cares how perfect the nature may be, how humble, how sweet, how gracious, that dwells in a chinless body? Nobody has time to inquire into natures, and the chinless must be content to be treated in something of the same good-natured, tolerant fashion in which we treat our poor relations until such time as they shall have grown a beard; and those who by their sex are forever shut out from this glorious possibility will have to take care, should they be of a bright intelligence, how they speak with the tongues of men and of angels, nothing being more droll than the effect of high words and poetic ideas issuing from a face that does not match them.

I wish we were not so easily affected by each other's looks. Sometimes, during the course of a long correspondence with a friend, he grows to be inexpressibly dear to me; I see how beautiful his soul is, how fine his intellect, how generous his heart, and how he already possesses in great perfection those qualities of kindness, and patience, and simplicity, after which I have been so long and so vainly striving. It is not I clothing him with the attributes I love and wandering away insensibly into that sweet land of illusions to which our footsteps turn whenever they are left to themselves, it is his very self unconsciously writing itself into his letters, the very man as he is without his body. Then I meet him again, and all illusions go. He is what I had always found him when we were together, good and amiable; but some trick of manner, some feature or attitude that I do not quite like, makes me forget, and be totally unable to remember, what I know from his letters to be true of him. He, no doubt, feels the same thing about me, and so between us there is a thick veil of something fixed, which, dodge as we may, we never can get round.

"Well, and what do you conclude from all that?" said the Man of Wrath, who had been going out by the verandah door with his gun and his dogs to shoot the squirrels before they had eaten up too many birds, and of whose coat-sleeve I had laid hold as he passed, keeping him by me like a second Wedding Guest, and almost as restless, while I gave expression to the above sentiments.

"I don't know," I replied, "unless it is that the world is very evil and the times are waxing late, but that doesn't explain anything either, because it isn't true."

And he went down the steps laughing and shaking his head and muttering something that I could not quite catch, and I am glad I could not, for the two words I did hear were women and nonsense.

He has developed an unexpected passion for farming, much to my relief, and though we came down here at first only tentatively for a year, three have passed, and nothing has been said about going back to town. Nor will anything be said so long as he is not the one to say it, for no three years of my life can come up to these in happiness, and not even those splendid years of childhood that grow brighter as they recede were more full of delights. The delights are simple, it is true, and of the sort that easily provoke a turning up of the worldling's nose; but who cares for noses that turn up? I am simple myself, and never tire of the blessed liberty from all restraints. Even such apparently indifferent details as being able to walk straight out of doors without first getting into a hat and gloves and veil are full of a subtle charm that is ever fresh, and of which I can never have too much. It is clear that I was born for a placid country life, and placid it certainly is; so much so that the days are sometimes far more like a dream than anything real, the quiet days of reading, and thinking, and watching the changing lights, and the growth and fading of the flowers, the fresh quiet days when life is so full of zest that you cannot stop yourself from singing because you are so happy, the warm quiet days lying on the grass in a secluded corner observing the procession of clouds–this being, I admit, a particularly undignified attitude, but think of the edification! Each morning the simple act of opening my bedroom windows is the means of giving me an ever-recurring pleasure. Just underneath them is a border of rockets in full flower, at that hour in the shadow of the house, whose gables lie sharply defined on the grass beyond, and they send up their good morning of scent the moment they see me leaning out, careful not to omit the pretty German custom of morning greeting. I call back mine, embellished with many endearing words, and then their fragrance comes up close, and covers my face with gentlest little kisses. Behind them, on the other side of the lawn on this west side of the house, is a thick hedge of lilac just now at its best, and what that best is I wish all who love lilac could see. A century ago a man lived here who loved his garden. He loved, however, in his younger years, travelling as well, but in his travels did not forget this little corner of the earth belonging to him, and brought back the seeds of many strange trees such as had never been seen in these parts before, and tried experiments with them in the uncongenial soil, and though many perished, a few took hold, and grew, and flourished, and shade me now at tea-time. What flowers he had, and how he arranged his beds, no one knows, except that the eleven beds round the sun-dial were put there by him; and of one thing he seems to have been inordinately fond, and that was lilac. We have to thank him for the surprising beauty of the garden in May and early June, for he it was who planted the great groups of it, and the banks of it, and massed it between the pines and firs. Wherever a lilac bush could go a lilac bush went; and not common sorts, but a variety of good sorts, white, and purple, and pink, and mauve, and he must have planted it with special care and discrimination, for it grows here as nothing else will, and keeps his memory, in my heart at least, forever gratefully green. On the wall behind our pew in church there is his monument, he having died here full of years, in the peace that attends the last hours of a good man who has loved his garden; and to the long Latin praises of his virtues and eminence I add, as I pass beneath it on Sundays, a heartiest Amen. Who would not join in the praises of a man to whom you owe your lilacs, and your Spanish chestnuts, and your tulip trees, and your pyramid oaks? "He was a good man, for he loved his garden"– that is the epitaph I would have put on his monument, because it gives one a far clearer sense of his goodness and explains it better than any amount of sonorous Latinities. How could he be anything *but* good since he loved a garden–that divine filter that filters all the grossness out of us, and leaves us, each time we have been in it, clearer, and purer, and more harmless?

June 16th.–Yesterday morning I got up at three o'clock and stole through the echoing passages and strange dark rooms, undid with trembling hands the bolts of the door to the verandah, and passed out into a wonderful, unknown world. I stood for a few minutes motionless on the steps, almost frightened by the awful purity of nature when all the sin and ugliness is shut up and asleep, and there is nothing but the beauty left. It was quite light, yet a bright moon hung in the cloudless grey-blue sky; the flowers were all awake, saturating the air with scent; and a nightingale sat on a hornbeam quite close to me, in loud raptures at the coming of the sun. There in front of me was the sun- dial, there were the rose bushes, there was the bunch of pansies I had dropped the night before still lying on the path, but how strange and unfamiliar it all looked, and how holy—as though God must be walking there in the cool of the day. I went down the path leading to the stream on the east side of the garden, brushing aside the rockets that were bending across it drowsy with dew, the larkspurs on either side of me rearing their spikes of heavenly blue against the steely blue of the sky, and the huge poppies like splashes of blood amongst the greys and blues and faint pearly whites of the innocent, new-born day. On the garden side of the stream there is a long row of silver birches, and on the other side a rye-field reaching across in powdery grey waves to the part of the sky where a solemn glow was already burning. I sat down on the twisted, half-fallen trunk of a birch and waited, my feet in the long grass and my slippers soaking in dew. Through the trees I could see the house with its closed shutters and drawn blinds, the people in it all missing, as I have missed day after day, the beauty of life at that hour. Just behind me the border of rockets and larkspurs came to an end, and, turning my head to watch a stealthy cat, my face brushed against a wet truss of blossom and got its first morning washing. It was wonderfully quiet, and the nightingale on the hornbeam had everything to itself as I sat motionless watching that glow in the east burning redder; wonderfully quiet, and so wonderfully beautiful because one associates daylight with people, and voices, and bustle, and hurryings to and fro, and the dreariness of working to feed our bodies, and feeding our bodies that we may be able to work to feed them again; but here was the world wide awake and yet only for me, all the fresh pure air only for me, all the fragrance breathed only by me, not a living soul hearing the nightingale but me, the sun in a few moments coming up to warm only me, and nowhere a single hard word being spoken, or a single selfish act being done, nowhere anything that could tarnish the blessed purity of the world as God has given it us. If one believed in angels one would feel that they must love us best when we are asleep and cannot hurt each other; and what a mercy it is that once in every twenty-four hours we are too utterly weary to go on being unkind. The doors shut, and the lights go out, and the sharpest tongue is silent, and all of us,

scolder and scolded, happy and unhappy, master and slave, judge
and culprit, are children again, tired, and hushed, and helpless,
and forgiven. And see the blessedness of sleep, that sends us
back for a space to our early innocence. Are not our first
impulses on waking always good? Do we not all know how in
times of wretchedness our first thoughts after the night's sleep
are happy? We have been dreaming we are happy, and we wake
with a smile, and stare still smiling for a moment at our stony
griefs before with a stab we recognise them.

There were no clouds, and presently, while I watched, the
sun came up quickly out of the rye, a great, bare, red ball, and
the grey of the field turned yellow, and long shadows lay upon
the grass, and the wet flowers flashed out diamonds. And then as
I sat there watching, and intensely happy as I imagined, suddenly
the certainty of grief, and suffering, and death dropped like a
black curtain between me and the beauty of the morning, and
then that other thought, to face which needs all our courage–the
realisation of the awful solitariness in which each of us lives and
dies. Often I could cry for pity of our forlornness, and of the
pathos of our endeavours to comfort ourselves. With what an
agony of patience we build up the theories of consolation that
are to protect, in times of trouble, our quivering and naked souls!
And how fatally often the elaborate machinery refuses to work at
the moment the blow is struck.

I got up and turned my face away from the unbearable,
indifferent brightness. Myriads of small suns danced before my
eyes as I went along the edge of the stream to the seat round the
oak in my spring garden, where I sat a little, looking at the
morning from there, drinking it in in long breaths, and
determining to think of nothing but just be happy. What a smell
of freshly mown grass there was, and how the little heaps into
which it had been raked the evening before sparkled with
dewdrops as the sun caught them. And over there, how hot the
poppies were already beginning to look–blazing back boldly in
the face of the sun, flashing back fire for fire. I crossed the wet
grass to the hammock under the beech on the lawn, and lay in it
awhile trying to swing in time to the nightingale's tune; and then
I walked round the ice-house to see how Goethe's corner looked

at such an hour; and then I went down to the fir wood at the bottom of the garden where the light was slanting through green stems; and everywhere there was the same mystery, and emptiness, and wonder. When four o'clock drew near I set off home again, not desiring to meet gardeners and have my little hour of quiet talked about, still less my dressing-gown and slippers; so I picked a bunch of roses and hurried in, and just as I softly bolted the door, dreadfully afraid of being taken for a burglar, I heard the first water-cart of the day creaking round the corner. Fearfully I crept up to my room, and when I awoke at eight o'clock and saw the roses in a glass by my side, I remembered what had happened as though it had been years ago.

Now here I have had an experience that I shall not soon forget, something very precious, and private, and close to my soul; a feeling as though I had taken the world by surprise, and seen it as it really is when off its guard—as though I had been quite near to the very core of things. The quiet holiness of that hour seems all the more mysterious now, because soon after breakfast yesterday the wind began to blow from the northwest, and has not left off since, and looking out of the window I cannot believe that it is the same garden, with the clouds driving over it in black layers, and angry little showers every now and then bespattering its harassed and helpless inhabitants, who cannot pull their roots up out of the ground and run for their lives, as I am sure they must long to do. How discouraging for a plant to have just proudly opened its loveliest flowers, the flowers it was dreaming about all the winter and working at so busily underground during the cold weeks of spring, and then for a spiteful shower of five minutes' duration to come and pelt them down, and batter them about, and cover the tender, delicate things with irremediable splashes of mud! Every bed is already filled with victims of the gale, and those that escape one shower go down before the next; so I must make up my mind, I suppose, to the wholesale destruction of the flowers that had reached perfection—that head of white rockets among them that washed my face a hundred years ago—and look forward cheerfully to the development of the younger generation of buds which cannot yet be harmed.

I know these gales. We get them quite suddenly, always from the north- west, and always cold. They ruin my garden for a day or two, and in the summer try my temper, and at all seasons try my skin; yet they are precious because of the beautiful clear light they bring, the intensity of cold blue in the sky and the terrific purple blackness of the clouds one hour and their divine whiteness the next. They fly screaming over the plain as though ten thousand devils with whips were after them, and in the sunny intervals there is nothing in any of nature's moods to equal the clear sharpness of the atmosphere, all the mellowness and indistinctness beaten out of it, and every leaf and twig glistening coldly bright. It is not becoming, a north-westerly gale; it treats us as it treats the garden, but with opposite results, roughly rubbing the softness out of our faces, as I can see when I look at the babies, and avoid the further proof of my own reflection in the glass. But there is life in it, glowing, intense, robust life, and when in October after weeks of serene weather this gale suddenly pounces on us in all its savageness, and the cold comes in a gust, and the trees are stripped in an hour, what a bracing feeling it is, the feeling that here is the first breath of winter, that it is time to pull ourselves together, that the season of work, and discipline, and severity is upon us, the stern season that forces us to look facts in the face, to put aside our dreams and languors, and show what stuff we are made of. No one can possibly love the summer, the dear time of dreams, more passionately than I do; yet I have no desire to prolong it by running off south when the winter approaches and so cheat the year of half its lessons. It is delightful and instructive to potter among one's plants, but it is imperative for body and soul that the pottering should cease for a few months, and that we should be made to realise that grim other side of life. A long hard winter lived through from beginning to end without shirking is one of the most salutary experiences in the world. There is no nonsense about it; you could not indulge in vapours and the finer sentiments in the midst of its deadly earnest if you tried. The thermometer goes down to twenty degrees of frost Reaumur, and down you go with it to the realities, to that elementary state where everything is big—health and sickness, delight and misery, ecstasy and despair. It makes you remember your poorer neighbours, and sends you into their homes to see that they too are fitted out with the armour of warmth and food necessary in the long fight; and in your own home it draws you nearer than ever to each other. Out of doors it is too cold to walk, so you run, and are rewarded by the conviction that you cannot be more than fifteen; or you get into your furs, and dart away in a sleigh over the snow, and are sure there never was music so charming as that of its bells; or you put on your skates, and are off to the lake to which you drove so often on June nights, when it lay rosy in the reflection of the northern glow, and all alive with myriads of wild duck and plovers, and which is now, but for the swish of your skates, so silent, and but for your warmth and jollity, so forlorn. Nor would I willingly miss the early darkness and the pleasant firelight tea and the long evenings among my books. It is then that I am glad I do not live in a cave, as I confess I have in my more godlike moments wished to do; it is then that I feel most capable of attending to the Man of Wrath's exhortations with an open mind; it is then that I actually like to hear the shrieks of the wind, and then that I give my heartiest assent, as I warm my feet at the fire, to the poet's proposition that all which we behold is full of blessings.

But what dreariness can equal the dreariness of a cold gale at midsummer? I have been chilly and dejected all day, shut up behind the streaming window-panes, and not liking to have a fire because of its dissipated appearance in the scorching intervals of sunshine. Once or twice my hand was on the bell and I was going to order one, when out came the sun and it was June again, and I ran joyfully into the dripping, gleaming garden, only to be driven in five minutes later by a yet fiercer squall. I wandered disconsolately round my pillar of books, looking for the one that would lend itself best to the task of entertaining me under the prevailing conditions, but they all looked gloomy, and reserved, and forbidding. So I sat down in a very big chair, and reflected that if there were to be many days like this it might be as well to ask somebody cheerful to come and sit opposite me in all those other big chairs that were looking so unusually gigantic and empty. When the Man of Wrath came in to tea there were such heavy clouds that the room was quite dark, and he peered about for a moment before he saw me. I suppose in the gloom of the big room I must have looked rather lonely, and smaller than usual buried in the capacious chair, for when he finally discovered me his face widened into an inappropriately cheerful smile.

"Well, my dear," he said genially, "how very cold it is."

"Did you come in to say that?" I asked.

"This tempest is very unusual in the summer," he proceeded; to which I made no reply of any sort.

"I did not see you at first amongst all these chairs and cushions. At least, I saw you, but it is so dark I thought you were a cushion."

Now no woman likes to be taken for a cushion, so I rose and began to make tea with an icy dignity of demeanour.

"I am afraid I shall be forced to break my promise not to invite any one here," he said, watching my face as he spoke. My heart gave a distinct leap—so small is the constancy and fortitude of woman. "But it will only be for one night." My heart sank down as though it were lead. "And I have just received a telegram that it will be to-night." Up went my heart with a cheerful bound.

"Who is it?" I inquired. And then he told me that it was the least objectionable of the candidates for the living here, made vacant by our own parson having been appointed superintendent, the highest position in the Lutheran Church; and the gale must have brought me low indeed for the coming of a solitary parson to give me pleasure. The entire race of Lutheran parsons is unpleasing to me,—whether owing to their fault or to mine, it would ill become me to say,—and the one we are losing is the only one I have met that I can heartily respect, and admire, and like. But he is quite one by himself in his extreme godliness, perfect simplicity, and real humility, and though I knew it was unlikely we should find another as good, and I despised myself for the eagerness with which I felt I was looking forward to seeing a new face, I could not stop myself from suddenly feeling cheerful. Such is the weakness of the female mind, and such the unexpected consequences of two months' complete solitude with forty-eight hours' gale at the end of them.

We have had countless applications during the last few weeks for the living, as it is a specially fat one for this part of the country, with a yearly income of six thousand marks, and a good house, and several acres of land. The Man of Wrath has been distracted by the difficulties of choice. According to the letters of recommendation, they were all wonderful men with unrivalled powers of preaching, but on closer inquiry there was sure to be some drawback. One was too old, another not old enough; another had twelve children, and the parsonage only allows for eight; one had a shrewish wife, and another was of Liberal tendencies in politics–a fatal objection; one was in money difficulties because he would spend more than he had, which was not surprising when one heard what he did have; and another was disliked in his parish because he and his wife were too close-fisted and would not spend at all; and at last, the Man of Wrath explained, the moment having arrived when if he did not himself appoint somebody his right to do so would lapse, he had written to the one who was coming, and invited him down that he might look at him, and ask him searching questions as to the faith which is in him.

I forgot my gloom, and my half-formed desperate resolve to break my vow of solitude and fill the house with the frivolous, as I sat listening to the cheerful talk of the little parson this evening. He was so cheerful, yet it was hard to see any cause for it in the life he was leading, a life led by the great majority of the German clergy, fat livings being as rare here as anywhere else. He told us with pleasant frankness all about himself, how he lived on an income of two thousand marks with a wife and six children, and how he was often sorely put to it to keep decent shoes on their feet. "I am continually drawing up plans of expenditure," he said, "but the shoemaker's bill is always so much more than I had expected that it throws my calculations completely out."

His wife, of course, was ailing, but already his eldest child, a girl of ten, took a great deal of the work off her mother's shoulders, poor baby. He was perfectly natural, and said in the simplest way that if the choice were to fall on him it would relieve him of many grinding anxieties; whereupon I privately determined that if the choice did not fall on him the Man of Wrath and I would be strangers from that hour.

"Have you been worrying him with questions about his principles?" I asked, buttonholing the Man of Wrath as he came out from a private conference with him.

"Principles? My dear Elizabeth, how can he have any on that income?"

"If he is not a Conservative will you let that stand in his way, and doom that little child to go on taking work off other people's shoulders?"

"My dear Elizabeth," he protested, "what has my decision for or against him to do with dooming little children to go on doing anything? I really cannot be governed by sentiment."

"If you don't give it to him–" and I held up an awful finger of warning as he retreated, at which he only laughed.

When the parson came to say good-night and good-bye, as he was leaving very early in the morning, I saw at once by his face that all was right. He bent over my hand, stammering out words of thanks and promises of devotion and invocations of blessings in such quantities that I began to feel quite pleased with myself, and as though I had been doing a virtuous deed. This feeling I saw reflected on the Man of Wrath's face, which made me consider that all we had done was to fill the living in the way that suited us best, and that we had no cause whatever to look and feel so benevolent. Still, even now, while the victorious candidate is dreaming of his trebled income and of the raptures of his home-coming to-morrow, the glow has not quite departed, and I am dwelling with satisfaction on the fact that we have been able to raise eight people above those hideous cares that crush all the colour out of the lives of the genteel poor. I am glad he has so many children, because there will be more to be made happy. They will be rich on the little income, and will no doubt dismiss the wise and willing eldest baby to appropriate dolls and pinafores; and everybody will have what they never yet have had, a certain amount of that priceless boon, leisure–leisure to sit down and look at themselves, and inquire what it is they really mean, and really want, and really intend to do with their lives. And this, I may observe, is a beneficial process wholly impossible on 100 pounds a year divided by eight.

But I wonder whether they will be thin-skinned enough ever to discover that other and less delightful side of life only seen by those who have plenty of leisure. Sordid cares may be very terrible to the sensitive, and make them miss the best of everything, but as long as they have them and are busy from morning till night keeping up appearances, they miss also the burden of those fears, and dreads, and realisations that beset him who has time to think. When in the morning I go into my sausage-room and give out sausages, I never think of anything but sausages. My horizon is bounded by them, every faculty is absorbed by them, and they engross me, while I am with them, to the exclusion of the whole world. Not that I love them; as far as that goes, unlike the effect they produce on most of my country-men, they leave me singularly cold; but it is one of my duties to begin the day with sausages, and every morning for the short time I am in the midst of their shining rows, watching my *Mamsell* dexterously hooking down the sleekest with an instrument like a boat-hook, I am practically dead to every other consideration in heaven or on earth. What are they to me, Love, Life, Death, all the mysteries? The one thing that concerns me is the due distribution to the servants of sausages; and until that is done, all obstinate questionings and blank misgivings must wait. If I were to spend my days in their entirety doing such work I should never have time to think, and if I never thought I should never feel, and if I never felt I should never suffer or rapturously enjoy, and so I should grow to be something very like a sausage myself, and not on that account, I do believe, any the less precious to the Man of Wrath.

I know what I would do if I were both poor and genteel— the gentility should go to the place of all good ilities, including utility, respectability, and imbecility, and I would sit, quite frankly poor, with a piece of bread, and a pot of geraniums, and a book. I conclude that if I did without the things erroneously supposed necessary to decency I might be able to afford a geranium, because I see them so often in the windows of cottages where there is little else; and if I preferred such inexpensive indulgences as thinking and reading and wandering in the fields to the doubtful gratification arising from kept- up appearances (always for the bedazzlement of the people opposite, and therefore always vulgar), I believe I should have enough left over to buy a radish to eat with my bread; and if the weather were fine, and I could eat it under a tree, and give a robin some crumbs in return for his cheeriness, would there be another creature in the world so happy? I know there would not.

The Garden Side *of the* Stream

JULY

J uly 1st.–I think that after roses sweet-peas are my favourite flowers. Nobody, except the ultra-original, denies the absolute supremacy of the rose. She is safe on her throne, and the only question to decide is which are the flowers that one loves next best. This I have been a long while deciding, though I believe I knew all the time somewhere deep down in my heart that they were sweet-peas; and every summer when they first come out, and every time, going round the garden, that I come across them, I murmur involuntarily, "Oh yes, *you* are the sweetest, you dear, dear little things." And what a victory this is, to be ranked next the rose even by one person who loves her garden. Think of the wonderful beauty triumphed over–the lilies, the irises, the carnations, the violets, the frail and delicate poppies, the magnificent larkspurs, the burning nasturtiums, the fierce marigolds, the smooth, cool pansies. I have a bed at this moment in the full glory of all these things, a little chosen plot of fertile land, about fifteen yards long and of irregular breadth, shutting in at its broadest the east end of the walk along the south front of the house, and sloping away at the back down to a moist, low bit by the side of a very tiny stream, or rather thread of trickling water, where, in the dampest corner, shining in the sun, but with their feet kept cool and wet, is a colony of Japanese irises, and next to them higher on the slope Madonna lilies, so chaste in looks and so voluptuous in smell, and then a group of hollyhocks in tenderest shades of pink, and lemon, and white, and right and left of these white marguerites and evening primroses and that most exquisite of poppies called Shirley, and a little on one side a group of metallic blue delphiniums beside a towering white lupin, and in and out and everywhere mignonette, and stocks, and pinks, and a dozen other smaller but not less lovely plants. I wish I were a poet, that I might properly describe the beauty of this bit as it sparkles this afternoon in the sunshine after rain; but of all the charming, delicate, scented groups it contains, none to my mind is so lovely as the group of sweet-peas in its north-west corner. There is something so utterly gentle and tender about sweet-peas, something so endearing in their clinging, winding, yielding growth; and then the long straight stalk, and the perfect little winged flower at the top, with its soft, pearly texture and wonderful range and combination of colours–all of them pure, all of them satisfying, not an ugly one, or even a less beautiful one among them. And in the house, next to a china bowl of roses, there is no arrangement of flowers so lovely as a bowl of sweet-peas, or a Delf jar filled with them. What a mass of glowing, yet delicate colour it is! How prettily, the moment you open the door, it seems to send its fragrance to meet you! And how you hang over it, and bury your face in it, and love it, and cannot get away from it. I really am sorry for all the people in the world who miss such keen pleasure. It is one that each person who opens his eyes and his heart may have; and indeed, most of the things that are really worth having are within everybody's reach. Anyone who chooses to take a country walk, or even the small amount of trouble necessary to get him on to his doorstep and make him open his eyes, may have them, and there are thousands of them thrust upon us by nature, who is forever giving and blessing, at every turn as we walk. The sight of the first pale flowers starring the copses; an anemone held up against the blue sky with the sun shining through it towards you; the first fall of snow in the autumn; the first thaw of snow in the spring; the blustering, busy winds blowing the winter away and scurrying the dead, untidy leaves into the corners; the hot smell of pines–just like blackberries–when the sun is on them; the first February evening that is fine enough to show how the days are lengthening, with its pale yellow strip of sky behind the black trees whose branches are pearled with raindrops; the swift pang of realisation that the winter is gone and the spring is coming;

the smell of the young larches a few weeks later; the bunch of cowslips that you kiss and kiss again because it is so perfect, because it is so divinely sweet, because of all the kisses in the world there is none other so exquisite—who that has felt the joy of these things would exchange them, even if in return he were to gain the whole world, with all its chimney-pots, and bricks, and dust, and dreariness? And we know that the gain of a world never yet made up for the loss of a soul.

One day, in going round the head inspector's garden with his wife, whose care it is, I remarked with surprise that she had no sweet-peas. I called them *Lathyrus odoratus*, and she, having little Latin, did not understand. Then I called them *wohlriechende Wicken*, the German rendering of that which sounds so pretty in English, and she said she had never heard of them. The idea of an existence in a garden yet without sweet-peas, so willing, so modest, and so easily grown, had never presented itself as possible to my imagination. Ever since I can remember, my summers have been filled with them; and in the days when I sat in my own perambulator and they were three times as tall as I was, I well recollect a certain waving hedge of them in the garden of my childhood, and how I stared up longingly at the flowers so far beyond my reach, inaccessibly tossing against the sky. When I grew bigger and had a small garden of my own, I bought their seeds to the extent of twenty pfennings, and trained the plants over the rabbit-hutch that was the chief feature in the landscape. There were other seeds in that garden seeds on which I had laid out all my savings and round which played my fondest hopes, but the sweet-peas were the only ones that came up. The same thing happened here in my first summer, my gardening knowledge not having meanwhile kept pace with my years, and of the seeds sown that first season sweet-peas again were the only ones that came up. I should say they were just the things for people with very little time and experience at their disposal to grow. A garden might be made beautiful with sweet-peas alone, and, with hardly any labour, except the sweet labour of picking to prolong the bloom, be turned into a fairy bower of delicacy and refinement. Yet the Frau Inspector not only had never heard of them, but, on my showing her a bunch, was not in the least impressed, and led me in her garden to a number of those exceedingly vulgar red herbaceous peonies growing among her currant bushes, and announced with conviction that they were her favourite flower. It was on the tip of my tongue to point out that in these days of tree-peonies, and peonies so lovely in their silvery faint tints that they resemble gigantic roses, it is absolutely wicked to suffer those odious red ones to pervert one's taste; that a person who sees nothing but those every time he looks out of his window very quickly has his nice perception for true beauty blunted; that such a person would do well to visit my garden every day during the month of May, and so get himself cured by the sight of my peony bushes covered with huge scented white and blush flowers; and that he would, I was convinced, at the end of the cure, go home and pitch his own on to the dust-heap. But of what earthly use would it have been? Pointing out the difference between what is beautiful and what misses beauty to a Frau Inspector of forty, whose chief business it is to make butter, is likely to be singularly unprolific of good results; and, further, experience has taught me that whenever anything is on the tip of my tongue the best thing to do is to keep it there. I wonder why a woman always wants to interfere.

It is a pity, nevertheless, that this lady should be so wanting in the aesthetic instinct, for her garden is full of possibilities. It lies due south, sheltered on the north, east, and west by farm buildings, and is rich in those old fruit-trees and well-seasoned gooseberry bushes that make such a good basis for the formation of that most delightful type of little garden, the flower-and-fruit-and-vegetable-mixed sort. She has, besides, an inestimable slimy, froggy pond, a perpetual treasure of malodorous water, much pined after by thirsty flowers; and then does she not live in the middle of a farmyard flowing with fertilising properties that only require a bucket and a shovel to transform them into roses? The way in which people miss their opportunities is melancholy.

This pond of hers, by the way, is an object of the liveliest interest to the babies. They do not seem to mind the smell, and they love the slime, and they had played there for several days in great peace before the unfortunate accident of the June baby's falling in and being brought back looking like a green and speckled frog herself, revealed where it was they had persuaded Seraphine to let them spend their mornings. Then there was woe and lamentation, for I was sure they would all have typhoid fever, and I put them mercilessly to bed, and dosed them, as a preliminary, with castor oil–that oil of sorrow, as Carlyle calls it. It was no use sending for the doctor because there is no doctor within reach; a fact which simplifies life amazingly when you have children. During the time we lived in town the doctor was never out of the house. Hardly a day passed but one or other of the Three had a spot, or, as the expressive German has it, a *Pickel*, and what parent could resist sending for a doctor when one lived round the corner? But doctors are like bad habits–once you have shaken them off you discover how much better you are without them; and as for the babies, since they inhabit a garden, prompt bed and the above-mentioned simple remedy have been all that is necessary to keep them robust. I admit I was frightened when I heard where they had been playing, for when the wind comes from that quarter even sitting by my rose beds I have been reminded of the existence of the pond; and I kept them in bed for three days, anxiously awaiting symptoms, and my head full of a dreadful story I had heard of a little boy who had drunk seltzer water and thereupon been seized with typhoid fever and had died, and if, I asked myself with a power of reasoning unusual in a woman, you die after seltzer water, what will you not do after frog-pond? But they did nothing, except be uproarious, and sing at the top of their voices, and clamour for more dinner than I felt would be appropriate for babies who were going to be dangerously ill in a few hours; and so, after due waiting, they were got up and dressed and turned loose again, and from that day to this no symptoms have appeared. The pond was at first strictly forbidden as a playground, but afterwards I made concessions, and now they are allowed to go to a deserted little burying-ground on the west side of it when the wind is in the west; and there at least they can hear the frogs, and sometimes, if they are patient, catch a delightful glimpse of them.

The graveyard is in the middle of a group of pines that bounds the Frau Inspector's garden on that side, and has not been used within the memory of living man. The people here love to make their little burying-grounds in the heart of a wood if they can, and they are often a long way away from the church to which they belong because, while every hamlet has its burying-ground, three or four hamlets have to share a church; and indeed the need for churches is not so urgent as that for graves, seeing that, though we may not all go to church, we all of us die and must be buried. Some of these little cemeteries are not even anywhere near a village, and you come upon them unexpectedly in your drives through the woods– bits of fenced-in forest, the old gates dropping off their hinges, the paths green from long disuse, the unchecked trees casting black, impenetrable shadows across the poor, meek, pathetic graves. I try sometimes, pushing aside the weeds, to decipher the legend on the almost speechless headstones; but the voice has been choked out of them by years of wind, and frost, and snow, and a few stray letters are all that they can utter–a last stammering protest against oblivion.

The Man of Wrath says all women love churchyards. He is fond of sweeping assertions, and is sometimes curiously feminine in his tendency to infer a general principle from a particular instance. The deserted little forest burying-grounds interest and touch me because they are so solitary, and humble, and neglected, and forgotten, and because so many long years have passed since tears were shed over the newly made graves. Nobody cries now for the husband, or father, or brother buried there; years and years ago the last tear that would ever be shed for them was dried–dried probably before the gate was reached on the way home–and they were not missed. Love and sorrow appear to be flowers of civilisation, and most to flourish where life has the broadest margin of leisure and abundance. The primary instincts are always there, and must first be satisfied; and if to obtain the means of satisfying them you have to work from morning till night without rest, who shall find time and energy to sit down and lament? I often go with the babies to the enclosure near the Frau Inspector's pond, and it seems just as natural that they should play there as that the white butterflies should chase each other undisturbed across the shadows. And then the place has a soothing influence on them, and they sober down as we approach it, and on hot afternoons sit quietly enough as close to the pond as they may, content to watch for the chance appearance of a frog while talking to me about angels.

This is their favourite topic of conversation in this particular place. Just as I have special times and places for certain books, so do they seem to have special times and places for certain talk. The first time I took them there they asked me what the mounds were, and by a series of adroit questions extracted the information that the people who had been buried there were now angels (I am not a specialist, and must take refuge in telling them what I was told in my youth), and ever since then they refuse to call it a graveyard, and have christened it the angel-yard, and so have got into the way of discussing angels in all their bearings, sometimes to my confusion, whenever we go there.

"But what *are* angels, mummy?" said the June baby inconsequently this afternoon, after having assisted at the discussions for several days and apparently listening with attention.

"*Such* a silly baby!" cried April, turning upon her with contempt, "don't you know they are *lieber Gott's* little girls?"

Now I protest I had never told those babies anything of the sort. I answer their questions to the best of my ability and as conscientiously as I can, and then, when I hear them talking together afterwards, I am staggered by the impression they appear to have received. They live in a whole world of independent ideas in regard to heaven and the angels, ideas quite distinct from other people's, and, as far as I can make out, believe that the Being they call *lieber Gott* pervades the garden, and is identical with, among other things, the sunshine and the air on a fine day. I never told them so, nor, I am sure, did Seraphine, and still less Seraphine's predecessor Miss Jones, whose views were wholly material; yet if, on bright mornings, I forget to immediately open all the library windows on coming down, the April baby runs in, and with quite a worried look on her face cries, "Mummy, won't you open the windows and let the *lieber Gott* come in?"

If they were less rosy and hungry, or if I were less prosaic, I might have gloomy forebodings that such keen interest in things and beings celestial was prophetic of a short life; and in books, we know, the children who talk much on these topics invariably die, after having given their reverential parents a quantity of advice. Fortunately such children are confined to books, and there is nothing of the ministering child–surely a very uncomfortable form of infant–about my babies. Indeed, I notice that in their conversations together on such matters a healthy spirit of contradiction prevails, and this afternoon, after having accepted April's definition of angels with apparent reverence, the June baby electrified the other two (always more orthodox and yielding) by remarking that she hoped she would never go to heaven. I pretended to be deep in my book and not listening; April and May were sitting on the grass sewing ("needling" they call it) fearful-looking woolwork things for Seraphine's birthday, and June was leaning idly against a pine trunk, swinging a headless doll round and round by its one remaining leg, her heels well dug into the ground, her sun-bonnet off, and all the yellow tangles of her hair falling across her sunburnt, grimy little face.

"No," she repeated firmly, with her eyes fixed on her sisters' startled faces, "I don't want to. There's nothing there for babies to play with."

"Nothing to play with?" exclaimed the other two in a breath–and throwing down their needle-work they made a simultaneous rush for me.

"Mummy, did you hear? June says she doesn't want to go into the *Himmel!*" cried April, horror-stricken.

"Because there's nothing to play with there, she says," cried May, breathlessly; and then they added with one voice, as though the subject had long ago been threshed out and settled between them, "Why, she can play at ball there with all the *Sternleins* if she likes!"

The idea of the June baby striding across the firmament and hurling the stars about as carelessly as though they were tennis-balls was so magnificent that it sent shivers of awe through me as I read.

"But if you break all your dolls," added April, turning severely to June, and eyeing the distorted remains in her hand, "I don't think *lieber Gott* will let you in at all. When you're big and have tiny Junes–real live Junes–I think you'll break them too, and *lieber Gott* doesn't love mummies what breaks their babies."

"But I *must* break my dolls," cried June, stung into indignation by what she evidently regarded as celestial injustice; "*lieber Gott* made me that way, so I can't help doing it, can I, mummy?"

On these occasions I keep my eyes fixed on my book, and put on an air of deep abstraction; and indeed, it is the only way of keeping out of theological disputes in which I am invariably worsted.

July 15th.–Yesterday, as it was a cool and windy afternoon and not as pleasant in my garden as it has lately been, I thought I would go into the village and see how my friends the farm hands were getting on. Philanthropy is intermittent with me as with most people, only they do not say so, and seize me like a cold in the head whenever the weather is chilly. On warm days my bump of benevolence melts away entirely, and grows bigger in proportion as the thermometer descends. When the wind is in the east it is quite a decent size, and about January, in a north-easterly snowstorm, it is plainly visible to the most casual observer. For a few weeks from then to the end of February I can hold up my head and look our parson in the face, but during the summer, if I see him coming my mode of progression in getting out of the way is described with perfect accuracy by the verb "to slink."

The village consists of one street running parallel to the outer buildings of the farm, and the cottages are one-storied, each with rooms for four families–two in front, looking on to the wall of the farmyard, which is the fashionable side, and two at the back, looking on to nothing more exhilarating than their own pigstyes. Each family has one room and a larder sort of place, and shares the kitchen with the family on the opposite side of the entrance; but the women prefer doing their cooking at the grate in their own room rather than expose the contents of their pots to the ill-natured comments of a neighbour. On the fashionable side there is a little fenced-in garden for every family, where fowls walk about pensively and meditate beneath the scarlet- runners (for all the world like me in my garden), and hollyhocks tower above the drying linen, and fuel, stolen from our woods, is stacked for winter use; but on the other side you walk straight out of the door on to manure heaps and pigs.

The street did not look very inviting yesterday, with a lowering sky above, and the wind blowing dust and bits of straw and paper into my face and preventing me from seeing what I knew to be there, a consoling glimpse of green fields and fir woods down at the other end; but I had not been for a long while—we have had such a lovely summer—and something inside me had kept on saying aggressively all the morning, "Elizabeth, don't you know you are due in the village? Why don't you go then? When are you going? Don't you know you *ought* to go? Don't you feel you *must*? Elizabeth, pull yourself together and *go*" Strange effect of a grey sky and a cool wind! For I protest that if it had been warm and sunny my conscience would not have bothered about me at all. We had a short fight over it, in which I got all the knocks, as was evident by the immediate swelling of the bump alluded to above, and then I gave in, and by two o'clock in the afternoon was lifting the latch of the first door and asking the woman who lived behind it what she had given the family for dinner. This, I was instructed on my first round by the Frau Inspector, is the proper thing to ask; and if you can follow it up by an examination of the contents of the saucepan, and a gentle sniff indicative of your appreciation of their savouriness, so much the better. I was diffident at first about this, but the gratification on their faces at the interest displayed is so unmistakable that I never now omit going through the whole business. This woman, the wife of one of the men who clean and feed the cows, has arrived at that enviable stage of existence when her children have all been confirmed and can go out to work, leaving her to spend her days in her clean and empty room in comparative dignity and peace. The children go to school till they are fourteen, then they are confirmed, are considered grown up, and begin to work for wages; and her three strapping daughters were out in the fields yesterday reaping. The mother has a keen, shrewd face, and everything about her was neat and comfortable. Her floor was freshly strewn with sand, her cups and saucers and spoons shone bright and clean from behind the glass door of the cupboard, and the two beds, one for herself and her husband and the other for her three daughters, were more mountainous than any I afterwards saw. The size and plumpness of her feather beds, the Frau Inspector tells me, is a woman's chief claim to consideration from the neighbours. She who can pile them up nearest to the ceiling becomes the principal personage in the community, and a flat bed is a social disgrace. It is a mystery to me, when I see the narrowness of the bedsteads, how so many people can sleep in them. They are rather narrower than what are known as single beds, yet father and mother and often a baby manage to sleep very well in one, and three or four children in the opposite corner of the room in another. The explanation no doubt is that they do not know what nerves are, and what it is to be wakened by the slightest sound or movement in the room and lie for hours afterwards, often the whole night, totally unable to fall asleep again, staring out into the darkness with eyes that refuse to shut. No nerves, and a thick skin—what inestimable blessings to these poor people! And they never heard of either.

I stood a little while talking, not asked to sit down, for that would be thought a liberty, and hearing how they had had potatoes and bacon for dinner, and how the eldest girl Bertha was going to be married at Michaelmas, and how well her baby was getting through its teething.

"Her baby?" I echoed, "I have not heard of a baby?"

The woman went to one of the beds and lifted up a corner of the great bag of feathers, and there, sure enough, lay a round and placid baby, sleeping as sweetly and looking as cherubic as the most legitimate of its contemporaries.

"And he is going to marry her at Michaelmas?" I asked, looking as sternly as I could at the grandmother.

"Oh yes," she replied, "he is a good young man, and earns eighteen marks a week. They will be very comfortable."

"It is a pity," I said, "that the baby did not make its appearance after Michaelmas instead of before. Don't you see yourself what a pity it is, and how everything has been spoilt?"

She stared at me for a moment with a puzzled look, and then turned away and carefully covered the cherub again. "They will be very comfortable," she repeated, seeing that I expected an answer; "he earns eighteen marks a week."

What was there to be said? If I had told her her daughter was a grievous sinner she might perhaps have felt transiently uncomfortable, but as soon as I had gone would have seen for herself, with those shrewd eyes of hers, that nothing had been changed by my denunciations, that there lay the baby, dimpled and healthy, that her daughter was making a good match, that none of her set saw anything amiss, and that all the young couples in the district had prefaced their marriages in this way.

Our parson is troubled to the depths of his sensitive soul by this custom. He preaches, he expostulates, he denounces, he implores, and they listen with square stolid faces and open mouths, and go back to their daily work among their friends and acquaintances, with no feeling of shame, because everybody does it, and public opinion, the only force that could stop it, is on their side. The parson looks on with unutterable sadness at the futility of his efforts; but the material is altogether too raw for successful manipulation by delicate fingers.

"Poor things," I said one day, in answer to an outburst of indignation from him, after he had been marrying one of our servants at the eleventh hour, "I am so sorry for them. It is so pitiful that they should always have to be scolded on their wedding day. Such children—so ignorant, so uncontrolled, so frankly animal—what do they know about social laws? They only know and follow nature, and I would from my heart forgive them all."

"It is *sin*" he said shortly.

"Then the forgiveness is sure."

"Not if they do not seek it."

I was silent, for I wished to reply that I believed they would be forgiven in spite of themselves, that probably they were forgiven whether they sought it or not, and that you cannot limit things divine; but who can argue with a parson? These people do not seek forgiveness because it never enters their heads that they need it. The parson tells them so, it is true, but they regard him as a person bound by his profession to say that sort of thing, and are sharp enough to see that the consequences of their sin, foretold by him with such awful eloquence, never by any chance come off. No girl is left to languish and die forsaken by her betrayer, for the betrayer is a worthy young man who marries her as soon as he possibly can; no finger of scorn is pointed at the fallen one, for all the fingers in the street are attached to women who began life in precisely the same fashion; and as for that problematical Day of Judgment of which they hear so much on Sundays, perhaps they feel that that also may be one of the things which after all do not happen.

The servant who had been married and scolded that morning was a groom, aged twenty, and he had met his little wife, she being then seventeen, in the place he was in before he came to us. She was a housemaid there, and must have been a pretty thing, though there were few enough traces of it, except the beautiful eyes, in the little anxious face that I saw for the first time immediately after the wedding, and just before the weary and harassed parson came in to talk things over. I had never heard of her existence until, about ten days previously, the groom had appeared, bathed in tears, speechlessly holding out a letter from her in which she said she could not bear things any longer and was going to kill herself. The wretched young man was at his wit's end, for he had not yet saved enough to buy any furniture and set up housekeeping, and she was penniless after so many months out of a situation. He did not know any way out of it, he had no suggestions to offer, no excuses to make, and just stood there helplessly and sobbed.

I went to the Man of Wrath, and we laid our heads together. "We do not want another married servant," he said.

"No, of course we don't," said I.

"And there is not a room empty in the village."

"No, not one."

"And how can we give him furniture? It is not fair to the other servants who remain virtuous, and wait till they can buy their own."

"No, certainly it isn't fair."

There was a pause.

"He is a good boy," I murmured presently.

"A very good boy."

"And she will be quite ruined unless somebody–"

"I'll tell you what we can do, Elizabeth," he interrupted; "we can buy what is needful and let him have it on condition that he buys it back gradually by some small monthly payment."

"So we can."

"And I think there is a room over the stables that is empty."

"So there is."

"And he can go to town and get what furniture he needs and bring the girl back with him and marry her at once. The sooner the better, poor girl."

And so within a fortnight they were married, and came hand in hand to me, he proud and happy, holding himself very straight, she in no wise yet recovered from the shock and misery of the last few hopeless months, looking up at me with eyes grown much too big for her face, eyes in which there still lurked the frightened look caught in the town where she had hidden herself, and where fingers of scorn could not have been wanting, and loud derision, and utter shame, besides the burden of sickness, and hunger, and miserable pitiful youth.

They stood hand in hand, she in a decent black dress, and both wearing very tight white kid gloves that refused to hide entirely the whole of the rough red hands, and they looked so ridiculously young, and the whole thing was so wildly improvident, that no words of exhortation would come to my lips as I gazed at them in silence, between laughter and tears. I ought to have told them they were sinners; I ought to have told them they were reckless; I ought to have told them by what a narrow chance they had escaped the just punishment of their iniquity, and instead of that I found myself stretching out hands that were at once seized and kissed, and merely saying with a cheerful smile, "*Nun Kinder, liebt Euch, und seid brav.*" And so they were dismissed, and then the parson came, in a fever at this latest example of deadly sin, while I, with the want of moral sense so often observable in woman, could only think with pity of their childishness. The baby was born three days later, and the mother very nearly slipped through our fingers; but she was a country girl, and she fought round, and by and by grew young again in the warmth of married respectability; and I met her the other day airing her baby in the sun, and holding her head as high as though she were conscious of a whole row of feather beds at home, every one of which touched the ceiling.

In the next room I went into an old woman lay in bed with her head tied up in bandages. The room had not much in it, or it would have been untidier; it looked neglected and gloomy, and some dirty plates, suggestive of long-past dinners, were piled on the table.

"Oh, such headaches!" groaned the old woman when she saw me, and moved her head from side to side on the pillow. I could see she was not undressed, and had crept under her feather bag as she was. I went to the bedside and felt her pulse–a steady pulse, with nothing of feverishness in it.

"Oh, such draughts!" moaned the old woman, when she saw I had left the door open.

"A little air will make you feel better," I said; the atmosphere in the shut-up room was so indescribable that my own head had begun to throb.

"Oh, oh!" she moaned, in visible indignation at being forced for a moment to breathe the pure summer air.

"I have something at home that will cure your headache," I said, "but there is nobody I can send with it to-day. If you feel better later on, come round and fetch it. I always take it when I have a headache"– ("Why, Elizabeth, you know you never have such things!" whispered my conscience, appalled. "You just keep quiet," I whispered back, "I have had enough of you for one day.")–"and I have some grapes I will give you when you come, so that if you possibly can, do."

"Oh, I can't move," groaned the old woman, "oh, oh, oh!" But I went away laughing, for I knew she would appear punctually to fetch the grapes, and a walk in the air was all she needed to cure her.

How the whole village hates and dreads fresh air! A baby died a few days ago, killed, I honestly believe, by the exceeding love of its mother, which took the form of cherishing it so tenderly that never once during its little life was a breath of air allowed to come anywhere near it. She is the watchman's wife, a gentle, flabby woman, with two rooms at her disposal, but preferring to live and sleep with her four children in one, never going into the other except for the christenings and funerals which take place in her family with what I cannot but regard as unnecessary frequency. This baby was born last September in a time of golden days and quiet skies, and when it was about three weeks old I suggested that she should take it out every day while the fine weather lasted. She pointed out that it had not yet been christened, and remembering that it is the custom in their class for both mother and child to remain shut up and invisible till after the christening, I said no more. Three weeks later I was its godmother, and it was safely got into the fold of the Church. As I was leaving, I remarked that now she would be able to take it out as much as she liked. The following March, on a day that smelt of violets, I met her near the house. I asked after the baby, and she began to cry. "It does not thrive," she wept, "and its arms are no thicker than my finger."

"Keep it out in the sun as much as you can," I said; "this is the very weather to turn weak babies into strong ones."

"Oh, I am so afraid it will catch cold if I take it out," she cried, her face buried in what was once a pocket-handkerchief.

"When was it out last?"

"Oh–" she stopped to blow her nose, very violently, and, as it seemed to me, with superfluous thoroughness. I waited till she had done, and then repeated my question.

"Oh–" a fresh burst of tears, and renewed exhaustive nose-blowing.

I began to suspect that my question, put casually, was of more importance than I had thought, and repeated it once more.

"I–can't t-take it out," she sobbed, "I know it–it would die."

"But has it not been out at all, then?"

She shook her head.

"Not once since it was born? Six months ago?"

She shook her head.

"*Poor* baby!" I exclaimed; and indeed from my heart I pitied the little thing, perishing in a heap of feathers, in one close room, with four people absorbing what air there was. "I am afraid," I said, "that if it does not soon get some fresh air it will not live. I wonder what would happen to my children if I kept them in one hot room day and night for six months. You see how they are out all day, and how well they are."

"They are so strong," she said, with a doleful sniff, "that they can stand it."

I was confounded by this way of looking at it, and turned away, after once more begging her to take the child out. She plainly regarded the advice as brutal, and I heard her blowing her nose all down the drive. In June the father told me he would like the doctor; the child grew thinner every day in spite of all the food it took. A doctor was got from the nearest town, and I went across to hear what he ordered. He ordered bottles at regular intervals instead of the unbroken series it had been having, and fresh air. He could find nothing the matter with it, except unusual weakness. He asked if it always perspired as it was doing then, and himself took off the topmost bag of feathers. Early in July it died, and its first outing was to the cemetery in the pine woods three miles off.

"I took such care of it," moaned the mother, when I went to try and comfort her after the funeral; "it would never have lived so long but for the care I took of it."

"And what the doctor ordered did no good?" I ventured to ask, as gently as I could.

"Oh, I did not take it out—how could I—it would have killed it at once—at least I have kept it alive till now." And she flung her arms across the table, and burying her head in them wept bitterly.

There is a great wall of ignorance and prejudice dividing us from the people on our place, and in every effort to help them we knock against it and cannot move it any more than if it were actual stone. Like the parson on the subject of morals, I can talk till I am hoarse on the subject of health, without at any time producing the faintest impression. When things are very bad the doctor is brought, directions are given, medicines made up, and his orders, unless they happen to be approved of, are simply not carried out. Orders to wash a patient and open windows are never obeyed, because the whole village would rise up if, later on, the illness ended in death, and accuse the relatives of murder. I suppose they regard us and our like who live on the other side of the dividing wall as persons of fantastic notions which, when carried into effect among our own children, do no harm because of the vast strength of the children accumulated during years of eating in the quantities only possible to the rich. Their idea of happiness is eating, and they naturally suppose that everybody eats as much as he can possibly afford to buy. Some of them have known hunger, and food and strength are coupled together in their experience—the more food the greater the strength; and people who eat roast meat (oh, bliss ineffable!) every day of their lives can bear an amount of washing and airing that would surely kill such as themselves. But how useless to try and discover what their views really are. I can imagine what I like about them, and am fairly certain to imagine wrong. I have no real conception of their attitude towards life, and all I can do is to talk to them kindly when they are in trouble, and as often as I can give them nice things to eat. Shocked at the horrors that must surround the poor women at the birth of their babies, I asked the Man of Wrath to try and make some arrangement that would ensure their quiet at those times. He put aside a little cottage at the end of the street as a home for them in their confinements, and I furnished it, and made it clean and bright and pretty. A nurse was permanently engaged, and I thought with delight of the unspeakable blessing and comfort it was going to be. Not a baby has been born in that cottage, for not a woman has allowed herself to be taken there. At the end of a year it had to be let out again to families, and the nurse dismissed.

"*Why* wouldn't they go?" I asked the Frau Inspector, completely puzzled. She shrugged her shoulders. "They like their husband and children round them," she said, "and are afraid something will be done to them away from home—that they will be washed too often, perhaps. The gracious lady will never get them to leave their homes."

"The gracious lady gives it up," I muttered.

When I opened the next door I was bewildered by the crowd in the room. A woman stood in the middle at a wash-tub which took up most of the space. Every now and then she put out a dripping hand and jerked a perambulator up and down for a moment, to calm the shrieks of the baby inside. On a wooden bench at the foot of one of the three beds a very old man sat and blinked at nothing. Crouching in a corner were two small boys of pasty complexion, playing with a guinea-pig and coughing violently. The loveliest little girl I have seen for a very long while lay in the bed nearest the door, quite silent, with her eyes closed and her mouth shut tight, as though she were trying hard to bear something. As I pulled the door open the first thing I saw, right up against it, was this set young face framed in tossed chestnut hair. "Why, *Frauchen*," I said to the woman at the tub, "so many of you at home to-day? Are you all ill?" There was hardly standing room for an extra person, and the room was full of steam.

"They have all got the cough I had," she answered, without looking up, "and Lotte there is very bad."

I took Lotte's rough little hand–so different from the delicate face– and found she was in a fever.

"We must get the doctor," I said.

"Oh, the doctor–" said the mother with a shrug, "he's no use."

"You must do what he tells you, or he cannot help you."

"That last medicine he sent me all but killed me," she said, washing vigorously. "I'll never take any more of his, nor shall any child of mine."

"What medicine was it?"

She wiped her hand on her apron, and reaching across to the cupboard took out a little bottle. "I was in bed two days after it," she said, handing it to me–"as though I were dead, not knowing what was going on round me." The bottle had contained opium, and there were explicit directions written on it as to the number of drops to be taken and the length of the intervals between the taking.

"Did you do exactly what is written here?" I asked.

"I took it all at once. There wasn't much of it, and I was feeling bad."

"But then of course it nearly killed you. I wonder it didn't quite. What good is it our taking all the trouble we do to send that long distance for the doctor if you don't do as he orders?"

"I'll take no more of his medicine. If it had been any good and able to cure me, the more I took the quicker I ought to have been cured." And she scrubbed and thumped with astounding energy, while Lotte lay with her little ashen face a shade more set and suffering. The wash-tub, though in the middle of the room, was quite close to Lotte's bed, because the middle of the room was quite close to every other part of it, and each extra hard maternal thump must have hit the child's head like a blow from a hammer. She was, you see, only thirteen, and her skin had not had time to turn into leather.

"Has this child eaten anything to-day?"

"She won't."

"Is she not thirsty?"

"She won't drink coffee or milk."

"I'll send her something she may like, and I shall send, too, for the doctor."

"I'll not give her his stuff."

"Let me beg you to do as he tells you."

"I'll not give her his stuff."

"Was it absolutely necessary to wash to-day?"

"It's the day."

"My good woman," said I to myself, gazing at her with outward blandness, "I'd like exceedingly to tip you up into your wash-tub and thump you as thoroughly as you are thumping those unfortunate clothes." Aloud I said in flute-like tones of conciliation, "Good afternoon."

"Good afternoon," said she without looking up.

Washing days always mean tempers, and I ought to have fled at the first sight of that tub, but then there was Lotte in her little yellow flannel night-gown, suffering as only children can suffer, helpless, forced to patience, forced to silent endurance of any banging and vehemence in which her mother might choose to indulge. No wonder her mouth was shut like a clasp and she would not open her eyes. Her eyebrows were reddish like her hair, and very straight, and her eyelashes lay dusky and long on her white face. At least I had discovered Lotte and could help her a little, I thought, as I departed down the garden path between the rows of scarlet-runners; but the help that takes the form of jelly and iced drinks is not of a lasting nature, and I have but little sympathy with a benevolence that finds its highest expression in gifts of the kind. There have been women within my experience who went down into the grave accompanied by special pastoral encomiums, and whose claims to lady-bountifulness, on closer inquiry, rested solely on a foundation of jelly. Yet nothing in the world is easier than ordering jelly to be sent to the sick, except refraining from ordering it. What more, however, could I do for Lotte than this? I could not take her up in my arms and run away with her and nurse her back to health, for she would probably object to such a course as strongly as her mother; and later on, when she gets well again, she will go back to school, and grow coarse and bouncing and leathery like the others, affording the parson, in three or four years' time, a fresh occasion for grief over deadly sin. "If one could only get hold of the children!" I sighed, as I went up the steps into the schoolhouse; "catch them young, and put them in a garden, with no older people of their own class for ever teaching them by example what is ugly, and unworthy, and gross."

Afternoon school was going on, and the assistant teacher was making the children read aloud in turns. In winter, when they would be glad of a warm, roomy place in which to spend their afternoons, school is only in the morning; and in summer, when the thirstiest after knowledge are apt to be less keen, it is both morning and afternoon. The arrangement is so mysterious that it must be providential. Herr Schenk, the head master, was away giving my babies their daily lessons, and his assistant, a youth in spectacles but yet of pugnacious aspect, was sitting in the master's desk, exercising a pretty turn for sarcasm in his running comments on the reading. A more complete waste of breath and brilliancy can hardly be imagined. He is not yet, however, married, and marriage is a great chastener. The children all stood up when I came in, and the teacher ceased sharpening his wits on a dulness that could not feel, and with many bows put a chair for me and begged me to sit on it. I did sit on it, and asked that they might go on with the lesson, as I had only come in for a minute on my way down the street. The reading was accordingly resumed, but unaccompanied this time by sarcasms. What faces! What dull, apathetic, low, coarse faces! On one side sat those from ten to fourteen, with not a hopeful face among them, and on the other those from six to ten, with one single little boy who looked as though he could have no business among the rest, so bright was he, so attentive, so curiously dignified. Poor children—what could the parson hope to make of beings whose expressions told so plainly of the sort of nature within? Those that did not look dull looked cunning, and all the girls on the older side had the faces of women. I began to feel dreadfully depressed. "See what you have done," I whispered angrily to my conscience—"made me wretched without doing anybody else any good." "The old woman with the headache is happy in the hopes of grapes," it replied, seeking to justify itself, "and Lotte is to have some jelly." "Grapes! Jelly! Futility unutterable. I can't bear this, and am going home." The teacher inquired whether the children should sing something to my graciousness; perhaps he was ashamed of their reading, and indeed I never heard anything like it. "Oh yes," I said, resigned, but outwardly smiling kindly with the self-control natural to woman. They sang, or rather screamed, a hymn, and so frightfully loud and piercingly that the very windows shook. "My dear," explained the Man of Wrath, when I complained one Sunday on our way home from church of the terrible quality and volume of the music, "it frightens Satan away."

Our numerous godchildren were not in school because, as we have only lived here three years, they are not yet old enough to share in the blessings of education. I stand godmother to the girls, and the Man of Wrath to the boys, and as all the babies are accordingly named after us the village swarms with tiny Elizabeths and Boys of Wrath. A hunchbacked woman, unfit for harder work, looks after the babies during the day in a room set apart for that purpose, so that the mothers may not be hampered in their duties at the farm; they have only to carry the babies there in the morning, and fetch them away again in the evening, and can feel that they are safe and well looked after. But many of them, for some reason too cryptic to fathom, prefer to lock them up in their room, exposed to all the perils that surround an inquiring child just able to walk, and last winter one little creature was burnt to death, sacrificed to her mother's stupidity. This mother, a fair type of the intelligence prevailing in the village, made a great fire in her room before going out, so that when she came back at noon there would still be some with which to cook the dinner, left a baby in a perambulator, and a little Elizabeth of three loose in the room, locked the door, put the key in her pocket, and went off to work. When she came back to get the dinner ready, the baby was still crowing placidly in its perambulator, and the little Elizabeth, with all the clothes burnt off her body, was lying near the grate dead. Of course the mother was wild with grief, distracted, raving, desperate, and of course all the other women were shocked and horrified; but point the moral as we might, we could not bring them to see that it was an avoidable misfortune with nothing whatever to do with the *Finger Gottes*, and the mothers who preferred locking their babies up alone to sending them to be looked after, went on doing so as undisturbed as though what had occurred could in no wise be a lesson to themselves. "Pray, *Herr Lehrer*, why are those two little boys sitting over there on that seat all by themselves and not singing?" I asked at the conclusion of the hymn.

"That, gracious lady, is the vermin bench. It is necessary to keep—"

"Oh yes, yes—I quite understand—good afternoon. Good-bye, children, you have sung very nicely indeed."

"Now," said I to myself, when I was safely out in the street again, "I am going home."

"Oh, not yet," at once protested my unmanageable conscience; "your favourite old woman lives in the next cottage, and surely you are not going to leave her out?"

"I see plainly," I replied, "that I shall never be quite comfortable till I have got rid of *you*" and in I went to the next house.

The entrance was full of three women—the entrances here are narrow, and the women wide—and they all looked more cheerful than seemed reasonable. They stood aside to let me pass, and when I opened the door I found the room equally full of women, looking equally happy, and talking eagerly.

"Why, what is happening?" I asked the nearest one. "Is there a party?"

She turned round, grinning broadly in obvious delight. "The old lady died in her sleep," she said, "and was found this morning dead in her bed. I was in here only yesterday, and she said—" I turned abruptly and went out again. All those gloating women, hovering round the poor body that was clothed on a sudden by death with a wonderful dignity and nobleness, made me ashamed of being a woman. Not a man was there,— clearly a superior race of beings. In the entrance I met the Frau Inspector coming in to arrange matters, and she turned and walked with me a little way.

"The old lady was better off than we thought," she remarked, "and has left a very good black silk dress to be buried in."

"A black silk dress?" I repeated.

"And everything to match in goodness—nice leather shoes, good stockings, under-things all trimmed with crochet, real whalebone corsets, and a quite new pair of white kid gloves. She must have saved for a long time to have it all so nice."

"But," I said, "I don't understand. I have never had anything to do yet with death, and have not thought of these things. Are not people, then, just buried in a shroud?"

"A shroud?" It was her turn not to understand.

"A sheet sort of thing."

She smiled in a highly superior manner. "Oh dear, no," she said, "we are none of us quite so poor as that."

I glanced down at her as she walked beside me. She is a short woman, and carries weight. She was smiling almost pityingly at my ignorance of what is due, even after death, to ourselves and public opinion.

"The very poorest," she said, "manage to scrape a whole set of clothes together for their funerals. A very poor couple came here a few months ago, and before the man had time to earn anything he died. The wife came to me (the gracious lady was absent), and on her knees implored me to give her a suit for him—she had only been able to afford the *Sterbehemd*, and was frantic at the thought of what the neighbours would say if he had nothing on but that, and said she would be haunted by shame and remorse all the rest of her life. We bought a nice black suit, and tie, and gloves, and he really looked very well. She will be dressed to-night," she went on, as I said nothing; "the dressers come with the coffin, and it will be a nice funeral. I used to wonder what she did with her pension money, and never could persuade her to buy herself a bit of meat. But of course she was saving for this. They are beautiful corsets."

"What utter waste!" I ejaculated.

"Waste?"

"Yes—utter waste and foolishness. Foolishness, not to have bought a few little comforts, waste of the money, and waste of the clothes. Is there any meaning, sense, or use whatever in burying a good black silk dress?"

"It would be a scandal not to be buried decently," she replied, manifestly surprised at my warmth, "and the neighbours respect her much more now that they know what nice clothes she had bought for her funeral. Nothing is wanting. I even found a box with a gold brooch in it, and a bracelet."

"I suppose, then, as many of her belongings as will go into the coffin will be buried too, in order to still further impress the neighbours?" I asked—"her feather bed, for instance, and anything else of use and value?"

"No, only what she has on, and the brushes and combs and towels that were used in dressing her."

"How ugly and how useless!" I said with a shiver of disgust.

"It is the custom," was her tranquil reply.

Suddenly an unpleasant thought struck me, and I burst out emphatically, "Nothing but a shroud is to be put on me."

"Oh no," she said, looking up at me with a face meant to be full of the most reassuring promises of devotion, "the gracious lady may be quite certain that if I am still here she will have on her most beautiful ball dress and finest linen, and that the whole neighbourhood shall see for themselves how well *Herrschaften* know what is due to them."

"I shall give directions," I repeated with increased energy, "that there is only to be a shroud."

"Oh no, no," she protested, smiling as though she were humouring a spoilt and eccentric child, "such a thing could never be permitted. What would our feelings be when we remembered that the gracious lady had not received her dues, and what would the neighbours say?"

"I'll have nothing but a shroud!" I cried in great wrath—and then stopped short, and burst out laughing. "What an absurd and gruesome conversation," I said, holding out my hand. "Good-bye, Frau Inspector, I am sure you are wanted in that cottage."

She made me a curtsey and turned back. I walked out of the village and through the fir wood and the meadow as quickly as I could, opened the gate into my garden, went down the most sheltered path, flung myself on the grass in a quiet nook, and said aloud "Ugh!"

It is a well-known exclamation of disgust, and is thus inadequately expressed in writing.

The South Part (1900)

August

August 5th.–August has come, and has clothed the hills with golden lupins, and filled the grassy banks with harebells. The yellow fields of lupins are so gorgeous on cloudless days that I have neglected the forests lately and drive in the open, so that I may revel in their scent while feasting my eyes on their beauty. The slope of a hill clothed with this orange wonder and seen against the sky is one of those sights which make me so happy that it verges on pain. The straight, vigorous flower- spikes are something like hyacinths, but all aglow with a divine intensity of brightness that a yellow hyacinth never yet possessed and never will; and then they are not waxy, but velvety, and their leaves are not futile drooping things, but delicate, strong sprays of an exquisite grey-green, with a bloom on them that throws a mist over the whole field; and as for the perfume, it surely is the perfume of Paradise. The plant is altogether lovely–shape, growth, flower, and leaf, and the horses have to wait very patiently once we get among them, for I can never have enough of sitting quite still in those fair fields of glory. Not far from here there is a low series of hills running north and south, absolutely without trees, and at the foot of them, on the east side, is a sort of road, chiefly stones, but yet with patience to be driven over, and on the other side of this road a plain stretches away towards the east and south; and hills and plain are now one sheet of gold. I have driven there at all hours of the day–I cannot keep away–and I have seen them early in the morning, and at mid-day, and in the afternoon, and I have seen them in the evening by moonlight, when all the intensity was washed out of the colour and into the scent; but just as the sun drops behind the little hills is the supreme moment, when the splendour is so dazzling that you feel as though you must have reached the very gates of heaven. So strong was this feeling the other day that I actually got out of the carriage, being impulsive, and began almost involuntarily to climb the hill, half expecting to see the glories of the New Jerusalem all spread out before me when I should reach the top; and it came with quite a shock of disappointment to find there was nothing there but the prose of potato-fields, and a sandy road with home-going calves kicking up its dust, and in the distance our neighbour's *Schloss*, and the New Jerusalem just as far off as ever.

It is a relief to me to write about these things that I so much love, for I do not talk of them lest I should be regarded as a person who rhapsodizes, and there is no nuisance more intolerable than having somebody's rhapsodies thrust upon you when you have no enthusiasm of your own that at all corresponds. I know this so well that I generally succeed in keeping quiet; but sometimes even now, after years of study in the art of holding my tongue, some stray fragment of what I feel does occasionally come out, and then I am at once pulled up and brought to my senses by the well-known cold stare of utter incomprehension, or the look of indulgent superiority that awaits any exposure of a feeling not in the least understood. How is it that you should feel so vastly superior whenever you do not happen to enter into or understand your neighbour's thoughts when, as a matter of fact, your not being able to do so is less a sign of folly in your neighbour than of incompleteness in yourself? I am quite sure that if I were to take most or any of my friends to those pleasant yellow fields they would notice nothing except the exceeding joltiness of the road; and if I were so ill-advised as to lift up a corner of my heart, and let them see how full it was of wonder and delight, they would first look blank, and then decide mentally that they were in the unpleasant situation of driving over a stony road with that worst form of idiot, a bore, and so fall into the mood of self- commiseration which is such a solace to us in our troubles. Yet it is painful being suppressed forever and ever, and I believe the torments of such a state, when unduly prolonged, are more keenly felt by a woman than a man, she having, in spite of her protestations, a good deal of the ivy nature still left in her, and an unhealthy craving for sympathy and support. When I drive to the lupins and see them all spread out as far as eye can reach in perfect beauty of colour and scent and bathed in the mild August sunshine, I feel I must send for somebody to come and look at them with me, and talk about them to me, and share in the pleasure; and when I run over the list of my friends and try to find one who would enjoy them, I am frightened once more at the solitariness in which we each of us live. I have, it is true, a great many friends— people with whom it is pleasant to spend an afternoon if such afternoons are not repeated often, and if you are careful not to stir more than the surface of things, but among them all there is only one who has, roughly, the same tastes that I have; and even her sympathies have limitations, and she declares for instance with emphasis that she would not at all like to be a goose-girl. I wonder why. Our friendship nearly came to an end over the goose-girl, so unexpectedly inflaming did the subject turn out to be. Of all professions, if I had liberty of choice, I would choose to be a gardener, and if nobody would have me in that capacity I would like to be a goose-girl, and sit in the greenest of fields minding those delightfully plump, placid geese, whiter and more leisurely than the clouds on a calm summer morning, their very waddle in its lazy deliberation soothing and salutary to a fretted spirit that has been too long on the stretch. The fields geese feed in are so specially charming, so green and low-lying, with little clumps of trees and bushes, and a pond or boggy bit of ground somewhere near, and a profusion of those delicate field flowers that look so lovely growing and are so unsatisfactory and fade so quickly if you try to arrange them in your rooms. For six months of the year I would be happier than any queen I ever heard of, minding the fat white things. I would begin in April with the king-cups, and leave off in September with the blackberries, and I would keep one eye on the geese, and one on the volume of Wordsworth I should have with me, and I would be present in this way at the procession of the months, the first three all white and yellow, and the last three gorgeous with the lupin fields and the blues and purples and crimsons that clothe the hedges and ditches in a wonderful variety of shades, and dye the grass near the water in great patches. Then in October I would shut up my Wordsworth, go back to civilised life, and probably assist at the eating of the geese one after the other, with a proper thankfulness for the amount of edification I had from first to last extracted from them.

I believe in England goose eating is held to be of doubtful refinement, and is left to one's servants. Here roast goose stuffed with apples is a dish loved quite openly and simply by people who would consider that the number of their quarterings raises them above any suspicion as to the refinement of their tastes, however many geese they may eat, and however much they may enjoy them; and I remember one lady, whose ancestors, probably all having loved goose, reached back up to a quite giddy antiquity, casting a gloom over a dinner table by removing as much of the skin or crackling of the goose as she could when it came to her, remarking, amidst a mournful silence, that it was her favourite part. No doubt it was. The misfortune was that it happened also to be the favourite part of the line of guests who came after her, and who saw themselves forced by the hard laws of propriety to affect an indifferent dignity of bearing at the very moment when their one feeling was a fierce desire to rise up and defend at all costs their right to a share of skin. She had, I remember, very pretty little white hands like tiny claws, and wore beautiful rings, and sitting opposite her, and free myself from any undue passion for goose, I had leisure to watch the rapid way in which she disposed of the skin, her rings and the whiteness of her hands flashing up and down as she used her knife and fork with the awful dexterity only seen in perfection in the Fatherland. I am afraid that as a nation we think rather more of our eating and drinking than is reasonable, and this no doubt explains why so many of us, by the time we are thirty, have lost the original classicality of our contour. Walking in the streets of a town you are almost sure to catch the word *essen* in the talk of the passers-by; and *das Essen*, combined, of course, with the drinking made necessary by its exaggerated indulgence, constitutes the chief happiness of the middle and lower classes.

Any story-book or novel you take up is full of feeling descriptions of what everybody ate and drank, and there are a great many more meals than kisses; so that the novel-reader who expects a love-tale, finds with disgust that he is put off with *menus*. The upper classes have so many other amusements that *das Essen* ceases to be one, and they are as thin as all the rest of the world; but if the curious wish to see how very largely it fills the lives, or that part of their lives that they reserve for pleasure, of the middle classes, it is a good plan to go to seaside places during the months of July and August, when the schools close, and the *bourgeoisie* realises the dream in which it has been indulging the whole year, of hotel life with a tremendous dinner every day at one o'clock.

The April baby was a weak little creature in her first years, and the doctor ordered as specially bracing a seaside resort frequented solely by the middle classes, and there for three succeeding years I took her; and while she rolled on the sands and grew brown and lusty, I was dull, and fell to watching the other tourists. Their time, it appeared, was spent in ruminating over the delights of the meal that was eaten, and in preparing their bodies by gentlest exercise for the delights of the meal that was to come. They passed their mornings on the sands, the women doing fancy work in order that they might look busy, and the men strolling aimlessly about near them with field-glasses, and nautical caps, and long cloaks of a very dreadful pattern reaching to their heels and making them look like large women, called Havelocks,–all of them waiting with more or less open eagerness for one o'clock, the great moment to which they had been looking forward ever since the day before, to arrive. They used to file in when the bell rang with a sort of silent solemnity, a contemplative collectedness, which is best described by the word *recueillement*, and ate all the courses, however many there were, in a hot room full of flies and sunlight.

The dinner lasted a good hour and a half, and at the end of that time they would begin to straggle out again, flushed and using toothpicks as they strolled to the tables under the trees, where the exhausted waiters would presently bring them breakfast-cups of coffee and cakes. They lingered about an hour over this, and then gradually disappeared to their rooms, where they slept, I suppose, for from then till about six a death-like stillness reigned in the place and April and I had it all to ourselves. Towards six, slow couples would be seen crawling along the path by the shore and panting up into the woods, this being the only exercise of the day, and necessary if they would eat their suppers with appreciation; and April and I, peering through the bracken out of the nests of moss we used to make in the afternoons, could see them coming up through the trees after the climb up the cliff, the husband with his Havelock over his arm, a little in front, wiping his face and gasping, the wife in her tight silk dress, her bonnet strings undone, a cloak and an umbrella, and very often a small mysterious basket as well to carry, besides holding up her dress, very stout and very uncomfortable and very breathless, panting along behind; and however much she had to carry, and however fat and helpless she was, and however steep the hill, and however much dinner she had eaten, the idea that her husband might have taken her cloak and her umbrella and her basket and carried them for her would never have struck either of them. If it had by some strange chance entered his head, he would have reasoned that he was as stout as she was, that he had eaten as much dinner, that he was several years older, and that it was her cloak. Logic is so irresistible.

To go on eating long after you have ceased to be hungry has fascinations, apparently, that are difficult to withstand, and if it gives you so much pleasure that the resulting inability to move without gasping is accepted with the meekness of martyrs, who shall say that you are wrong? My not myself liking a large dinner at one o'clock is not a reason for my thinking I am superior to those who do. Their excesses, it is true, are not my excesses, but then neither are mine theirs; and what about the days of idleness I spend, doing nothing from early till late but lie on the grass watching clouds? If I were to murmur gluttons, could not they, from their point of view, retort with conviction fool? All those maxims about judging others by yourself, and putting yourself in another person's place, are not, I am afraid, reliable. I had them dinned into me constantly as a child, and I was constantly trying to obey them, and constantly was astonished at the unexpected results I arrived at; and now I know that it is a proof of artlessness to suppose that other people will think and feel and hope and enjoy what you do and in the same way that you do. If an officious friend had stood in that breathless couple's path and told them in glowing terms how much happier they would be if they lived their life a little more fully and from its other sides, how much more delightful to stride along gaily together in their walks, with wind enough for talk and laughter, how pleasant if the man were muscular and in good condition and the woman brisk and wiry, and that they only had to do as he did and live on cold meat and toast, and drink nothing, to be as blithe as birds, do you think they would have so much as understood him? Cold meat and toast? Instead of what they had just been enjoying so intensely? Miss that soup made of the inner mysteries of geese, those eels stewed in beer, the roast pig with red cabbage, the venison basted with sour cream and served with beans in vinegar and cranberry jam, the piled-up masses of vanilla ice, the pumpernickel and cheese, the apples and pears on the top of that, and the big cups of coffee and cakes on the top of the apples and pears? Really a quick walk over the heather with a wiry wife would hardly make up for the loss of such a dinner; and besides, might not a wiry wife turn out to be a questionable blessing? And so they would pity the nimble friend who wasted his life in taking exercise and missed all its pleasures, and the man of toast and early rising would regard them with profound disgust if simple enough to think himself better than they, and, if he possessed an open mind, would merely return their pity with more of his own; so that, I suppose, everybody would be pleased, for the charm of pitying one's neighbour, though subtle, is undeniable.

I remember when I was at the age when people began to call me *Backfisch*, and my mother dressed me in a little scarlet coat with big pearl buttons, and my eyes turned down because I was shy, and my nose turned up because I was impudent, one summer at the seaside with my governess we noticed in our walks a solitary lady of dignified appearance, who spoke to no one, and seemed for ever wrapped in distant and lofty philosophic speculations. "She's thinking about Kant and the nebular hypothesis," I decided to myself, having once heard some men with long beards talking of both those things, and they all had had that same far-away look in their eyes. "*Qu'est-ce que c'est une hypothese nebuleuse, Mademoiselle?*" I said aloud.

"*Tenez-vous bien, et marchez d'une façon convenable,*" she replied sharply.

"*Qu'est-ce que c'est une hypothese—*"

"*Vous etes trop jeune pour comprendre ces choses.*"

"*Oh alors vous ne savez pas vous-meme!*" I cried triumphantly, "*Sans cela vous me diriez.*"

"*Elisabeth, vous ecrirez, des que nous rentrons, le verbe Prier le bon Dieu de m'Aider a ne plus Etre si Impertinente.*"

She was an ingenious young woman, and the verbs I had to write as punishments were of the most elaborate and complicated nature— *Demander pardon pour Avoir Siffle comme un Gamin quelconque, Vouloir ne plus Oublier de Nettoyer mes Ongles, Essayer de ne pas tant Aimer les Poudings,* are but a few examples of her achievements in this particular branch of discipline.

That very day at the *table d'hote* the abstracted lady sat next to me. A *ragout* of some sort was handed round, and after I had taken some she asked me, before helping herself, what it was.

"Snails," I replied promptly, wholly unchastened by the prayers I had just been writing out in every tense.

"Snails! *Ekelig.*" And she waved the waiter loftily away, and looked on with much superciliousness at the rest of us enjoying ourselves.

"What! You do not eat this excellent *ragout?*" asked her other neighbour, a hot man, as he finished clearing his plate and had time to observe the emptiness of hers. "You do not like calves' tongues and mushrooms? *Sonderbar.*"

I still can see the poor lady's face as she turned on me more like a tigress than the impassive person she had been a moment before. "*Sie unverschamter Backfisch!*" she hissed. "My favourite dish—I have you to thank for spoiling my repast—my day!" And in a frenzy of rage she gripped my arm as though she would have shaken me then and there in the face of the multitude, while I sat appalled at the consequences of indulging a playful fancy at the wrong time.

Which story, now I come to think of it, illustrates less the tremendous importance of food in our country than the exceeding odiousness of *Backfisch* in scarlet coats.

August 10th.–My idea of a garden is that it should be beautiful from end to end, and not start off in front of the house with fireworks, going off at its farthest limit into sheer sticks. The standard reached beneath the windows should at least be kept up, if it cannot be surpassed, right away through, and the German popular plan in this matter quite discarded of concentrating all the available splendour of the establishment into the supreme effort of carpet-bedding and glass balls on pedestals in front of the house, in the hope that the stranger, carefully kept in that part, and on no account allowed to wander, will infer an equal magnificence throughout the entire domain; whereas he knows very well all the time that the landscape round the corner consists of fowls and dust-bins. Disliking this method, I have tried to make my garden increase in loveliness, if not in tidiness, the farther you get into it; and the visitor who thinks in his innocence as he emerges from the shade of the verandah that he sees the best before him, is artfully conducted from beauty to beauty till he beholds what I think is the most charming bit, the silver birch and azalea plantation down at the very end. This is the boundary of my kingdom on the south side, a blaze of colour in May and June, across which you see the placid meadows stretching away to a distant wood; and from its contemplation the ideal visitor returns to the house a refreshed and better man. That is the sort of person one enjoys taking round–the man (or woman) who, loving gardens, would go any distance to see one; who comes to appreciate, and compare, and admire; who has a garden of his own that he lives in and loves; and whose talk and criticisms are as dew to the thirsty gardening soul, all too accustomed in this respect to droughts. He knows as well as I do what work, what patience, what study and watching, what laughter at failures, what fresh starts with undiminished zeal, and what bright, unalterable faith are represented by the flowers in my garden. He knows what I have done for it, and he knows what it has done for me, and how it has been and will be more and more a place of joys, a place of lessons, a place of health, a place of miracles, and a place of sure and never-changing peace.

Living face to face with nature makes it difficult for one to be discouraged. Moles and late frosts, both of which are here in abundance, have often grieved and disappointed me, but even these, my worst enemies, have not succeeded in making me feel discouraged. Not once till now have I got farther in that direction than the purely negative state of not being encouraged; and whenever I reach that state I go for a brisk walk in the sunshine and come back cured. It makes one so healthy to live in a garden, so healthy in mind as well as body, and when I say moles and late frosts are my worst enemies, it only shows how I could not now if I tried sit down and brood over my own or my neighbour's sins, and how the breezes in my garden have blown away all those worries and vexations and bitternesses that are the lot of those who live in a crowd. The most severe frost that ever nipped the hopes of a year is better to my thinking than having to listen to one malignant truth or lie, and I would rather have a mole busy burrowing tunnels under each of my rose trees and letting the air get at their roots than face a single greeting where no kindness is. How can you help being happy if you are healthy and in the place you want to be? A man once made it a reproach that I should be so happy, and told me everybody has crosses, and that we live in a vale of woe. I mentioned moles as my principal cross, and pointed to the huge black mounds with which they had decorated the tennis-court, but I could not agree to the vale of woe, and could not be shaken in my belief that the world is a dear and lovely place, with everything in it to make us happy so long as we walk humbly and diet ourselves. He pointed out that sorrow and sickness were sure to come, and seemed quite angry with me when I suggested that they too could be borne perhaps with cheerfulness. "And have not even such things their sunny side?" I exclaimed. "When I am steeped to the lips in diseases and doctors, I shall at least have something to talk about that interests my women friends, and need not sit as I do now wondering what I shall say next and wishing they would go." He replied that all around me lay misery, sin, and suffering, and that every person not absolutely blinded by selfishness must be aware of it and must realise the seriousness and tragedy of existence. I asked him whether my being miserable and discontented would help anyone or make him less wretched; and he said that we all had to take up our burdens. I assured him I would not shrink from mine, though I felt secretly ashamed of it when I remembered that it was only moles, and he went away with a grave face and a shaking head, back to his wife and his eleven children. I heard soon afterwards that a twelfth baby had been born and his wife had died, and in dying had turned her face with a quite unaccountable impatience away from him and to the wall; and the rumour of his piety reached even into my garden, and how he had said, as he closed her eyes, "It is the Will of God." He was a missionary.

But of what use is it telling a woman with a garden that she ought really to be ashamed of herself for being happy? The fresh air is so buoyant that it lifts all remarks of that sort away off you and leaves you laughing. They get wafted away on the scent of the stocks, and you stand in the sun looking round at your cheerful flowers, and more than ever persuaded that it is a good and blessed thing to be thankful. Oh a garden is a sweet, sane refuge to have! Whether I am tired because I have enjoyed myself too much, or tired because I have lectured the servants too much, or tired because I have talked to missionaries too much, I have only to come down the verandah steps into the garden to be at once restored to quiet, and serenity, and my real and natural self. I could almost fancy sometimes that as I come down the steps, gentle hands of blessing have been laid on my head. I suppose I feel so because of the hush that descends on my soul when I get out of the close, restless house into that silent purity. Sometimes I sit for hours in the south walk by the verandah just listening and watching. It is so private there, though directly beneath the windows, that it is one of my favourite places. There are no bedrooms on that side of the house, only the Man of Wrath's and my day-rooms, so that servants cannot see me as I stand there enjoying myself. If they did or could, I should simply never go there, for nothing is so utterly destructive to meditation as to know that probably somebody inquisitive is eyeing you from behind a curtain. The loveliest garden I know is spoilt to my thinking by the impossibility of getting out of sight of the house, which stares down at you, Argus-eyed and unblinking, into whatever corner you may shuffle. Perfect house and perfect garden, lying in that land of lovely gardens, England, the garden just the right size for perfection, not a weed ever admitted, every dandelion and daisy– those friends of the unaspiring– routed out years ago, the borders exquisite examples of taste, the turf so faultless that you hardly like to walk on it for fear of making it dusty, and the whole quite uninhabitable for people of my solitary tendencies because, go where you will, you are overlooked. Since I have lived in this big straggling place, full of paths and copses where I am sure of being left alone, with wide fields and heath and forests beyond, and so much room to move and breathe in, I feel choked, oppressed, suffocated, in anything small and perfect. I spent a very happy afternoon in that little English paradise, but I came away quite joyfully, and with many a loving thought of my own dear ragged garden, and all the corners in it where the anemones twinkle in the spring like stars, and where there is so much nature and so little art. It will grow I know sweeter every year, but it is too big ever to be perfect and to get to look so immaculate that the diseased imagination conjures up visions of housemaids issuing forth each morning in troops and dusting every separate flower with feather brushes. Nature herself is untidy, and in a garden she ought to come first, and Art with her brooms and clipping-shears follow humbly behind. Art has such a good time in the house, where she spreads herself over the walls, and hangs herself up gorgeously at the windows, and lurks in the sofa cushions, and breaks out in an eruption of pots wherever pots are possible, that really she should be content to take the second place out of doors. And how dreadful to meet a gardener and a wheelbarrow at every turn–which is precisely what happens to one in the perfect garden. My gardener, whose deafness is more than compensated for by the keenness of his eyesight, very soon remarked the scowl that distorted my features whenever I met one of his assistants in my favourite walks, and I never meet them now. I think he must keep them chained up to the cucumber-frames, so completely have they disappeared, and he only lets them loose when he knows I am driving, or at meals, or in bed. But is it not irritating to be sitting under your favourite tree, pencil in hand, and eyes turned skywards expectant of the spark from heaven that never falls, and then to have a man appear suddenly round the corner who immediately begins quite close to you to tear up the earth with his fangs? No one will ever know the number of what I believe are technically known as winged words that I have missed bringing down through interruptions of this kind. Indeed, as I look through these pages I see I must have missed them all, for I can find nothing anywhere with even a rudimentary approach to wings.

Sometimes when I am in a critical mood and need all my faith to keep me patient, I shake my head at the unshornness of the garden as gravely as the missionary shook his head at me. The bushes stretch across the paths, and, catching at me as I go by, remind me that they have not been pruned; the teeming plant life rejoices on the lawns free from all interference from men and hoes; the pinks are closely nibbled off at the beginning of each summer by selfish hares intent on their own gratification; most of the beds bear the marks of nocturnal foxes; and the squirrels spend their days wantonly biting off and flinging down the tender young shoots of the firs. Then there is the boy who drives the donkey and water-cart round the garden, and who has an altogether reprehensible habit of whisking round corners and slicing off bits of the lawn as he whisks. "But you can't alter these things, my good soul," I say to myself. "If you want to get rid of the hares and foxes, you must consent to have wire-netting, which is odious, right round your garden. And you are always saying you like weeds, so why grumble at your lawns? And it doesn't hurt you much if the squirrels do break bits off your firs—the firs must have had that happening to them years and years before you were born, yet they still flourish. As for boys, they certainly are revolting creatures. Can't you catch this one when he isn't looking and pop him in his own water-barrel and put the lid on?"

I asked the June baby, who had several times noticed with indignation the culpable indifference of this boy in regard to corners, whether she did not think that would be a good way of disposing of him. She is a great disciplinarian, and was loud in her praise of the plan; but the other two demurred. "He might go dead in there," said the May baby, apprehensively. "And he is such a naughty boy," said April, who had watched his reckless conduct with special disgust, "that if he once went dead he'd go straight to the *Holle* and stay all the time with the *diable*."

That was the first French word I have heard them say: strange and sulphureous first-fruits of Seraphine's teaching!

We were going round the garden in a procession, I with a big pair of scissors, and the Three with baskets, into one of which I put fresh flowers, and into the others flowers that were beginning to seed, dead flowers, and seed-pods. The garden was quivering in heat and light; rain in the morning had brought out all the snails and all the sweetness, and we were very happy, as we always are, I when I am knee-deep in flowers, and the babies when they can find new sorts of snails to add to their collections. These collections are carried about in cardboard boxes all day, and at night each baby has hers on the chair beside her bed. Sometimes the snails get out and crawl over the beds, but the babies do not mind. Once when April woke in the morning she was overjoyed by finding a friendly little one on her cheek. Clearly babies of iron nerves and pellucid consciences.

"So you do know some French," I said as I snipped off poppy-heads; "you have always pretended you don't."

"Oh, keep the poppies, mummy," cried April, as she saw them tumbling into her basket; "if you picks them and just leaves them, then they ripes and is good for such a many things."

"Tell me about the *diable*," I said, "and you shall keep the poppies."

"He isn't nice, that *diable*," she said, starting off at once with breathless eloquence. "Seraphine says there was one time a girl and a boy who went for a walk, and there were two ways, and one way goes where stones is, but it goes to the *lieber Gott*; and the girl went that way till she came to a door, and the *lieber Gott* made the door opened and she went in, and that's the *Himmel.*"

"And the boy?"

"Oh, he was a naughty boy and went the other way where there is a tree, and on the tree is written, 'Don't go this way or you'll be dead,' and he said, 'That is one *betise,*' and did go in the way and got to the *Holle*, and there he gets whippings when he doesn't make what the *diable* says."

"That's because he was so naughty," explained the May baby, holding up an impressive finger, "and didn't want to go to the *Himmel* and didn't love glory."

"All boys are naughty," said June, "and I don't love them."

"*Nous allons parler Francais*" I announced, desirous of finding out whether their whole stock was represented by *diable* and *betise*; "I believe you can all speak it quite well."

There was no answer. I snipped off sweet-pea pods and began to talk French at a great rate, asking questions as I snipped, and trying to extract answers, and getting none. The silence behind me grew ominous. Presently I heard a faint sniff, and the basket being held up to me began to shake. I bent down quickly and looked under April's sun-bonnet. She was crying great dreadful tears, and rubbing her eyes hard with her one free hand.

"Why, you most blessed of babies," I exclaimed, kneeling down and putting my arms round her, "what in the world is the matter?"

She looked at me with grieved and doubting eyes. "Such a mother to talk French to her child!" she sobbed.

I threw down the scissors, picked her up, and carried her up and down the path, comforting her with all the soft words I knew and suppressing my desire to smile. "That's not French, is it?" I whispered at the end of a long string of endearments, beginning, I believe, with such flights of rhetoric as priceless blessing and angel baby, and ending with a great many kisses.

"No, no," she answered, patting my face and looking infinitely relieved, "that is pretty, and how mummies always talks. Proper mummies never speak French—only Seraphines." And she gave me a very tight hug, and a kiss that transferred all her tears to my face; and I set her down and, taking out my handkerchief, tried to wipe off the traces of my attempt at governessing from her cheeks. I wonder how it is that whenever babies cry, streaks of mud immediately appear on their faces. I believe I could cry for a week, and yet produce no mud.

"I'll tell you what I'll do, babies," I said, anxious to restore complete serenity on such a lovely day, and feeling slightly ashamed of my uncalled-for zeal—indeed, April was right, and proper mothers leave lessons and torments to somebody else, and devote all their energies to petting—"I'll give a ball after tea."

"*Yes!*" shouted three exultant voices, "and invite all the babies!"

"So now you must arrange what you are going to wear. I suppose you'd like the same supper as usual? Run away to Seraphine and tell her to get you ready."

They seized their baskets and their boxes of snails and rushed off into the bushes, calling for Seraphine with nothing but rapture in their voices, and French and the *diable* quite forgotten.

These balls are given with great ceremony two or three times a year. They last about an hour, during which I sit at the piano in the library playing cheerful tunes, and the babies dance passionately round the pillar. They refuse to waltz together, which is perhaps a good thing, for if they did there would always be one left over to be a wallflower and gnash her teeth; and when they want to dance squares they are forced by the stubbornness of numbers to dance triangles. At the appointed hour they knock at the door, and come in attired in the garments they have selected as appropriate (at this last ball the April baby wore my shooting coat, the May baby had a muff, and the June baby carried Seraphine's umbrella), and, curtseying to me, each one makes some remark she thinks suitable to the occasion.

"How's your husband?" June asked me last time, in the defiant tones she seems to think proper at a ball.

"Very well, thank you."

"Oh, that is nice."

"Mine isn't vely well," remarked April, cheerfully.

"Indeed?"

"No, he has got some tummy-aches."

"Dear me!"

"He was coming else, and had such fine twowsers to wear—pink ones with wibbons."

After a little more graceful conversation of this kind the ball begins, and at the end of an hour's dancing, supper, consisting of radishes and lemonade, is served on footstools; and when they have cleared it up even to the leaves and stalks of the radishes, they rise with much dignity, express in proper terms their sense of gratitude for the entertainment, curtsey, and depart to bed, where they spend a night of horror, the prey of the awful dreams naturally resulting from so unusual a combination as radishes and babies. That is why my balls are rare festivals—the babies will insist on having radishes for the supper, and I, as a decent parent with a proper sense of my responsibilities, am forced accordingly to restrict my invitations to two, at the most three, in a year.

When this last one was over I felt considerably exhausted, and had hardly sufficient strength to receive their thanks with civility. An hour's jig-playing with the thermometer at 90 leaves its marks on the most robust; and when they were in bed, and the supper beginning to do its work, I ordered the carriage and the kettle with a view to seeking repose in the forest, taking the opportunity of escaping before the Man of Wrath should come in to dinner. The weather has been very hot for a long time, but the rain in the morning had had a wonderful effect on my flowers, and as I drove away I could not help noticing how charming the borders in front of the house were looking, with their white hollyhocks, and white snapdragons, and fringe of feathery marigolds. This gardener has already changed the whole aspect of the place, and I believe I have found the right man at last. He is very young for a head gardener, but on that account all the more anxious to please me and keep his situation; and it is a great comfort to have to do with somebody who watches and interprets rightly every expression of one's face and does not need much talking to. He makes mistakes sometimes in the men he engages, just as I used to when I did the engaging, and he had one poor young man as apprentice who very soon, like the first of my three meek gardeners, went mad. His madness was of a harmless nature and took a literary form; indeed, that was all they had against him, that he would write books. He used to sit in the early morning on my special seats in the garden, and strictly meditate the thankless muse when he ought to have been carting manure; and he made his fellow-apprentices unspeakably wretched by shouting extracts from Schiller at them across the intervening gooseberry bushes. Let me hasten to say that I had never spoken to him, and should not even have known what he was like if he had not worn eyeglasses, so that the Man of Wrath's insinuation that I affect the sanity of my gardeners is entirely without justification. The eyeglasses struck me as so odd on a gardener that I asked who he was, and was told that he had been studying for the Bar, but could not pass the examinations, and had taken up gardening in the hope of getting back his health and spirits. I thought this a very sensible plan, and was beginning to feel interested in him when one day the post brought me a registered packet containing a manuscript play he had written called "The Lawyer as Gardener," dedicated to me. The Man of Wrath and I were both in it, the Man of Wrath, however, only in the list of characters, so that he should not feel hurt, I suppose, for he never appeared on the scenes at all. As for me, I was represented as going about quoting Tolstoi in season and out of season to the gardeners—a thing I protest I never did. The young man was sent home to his people, and I have been asking myself ever since what there is about this place that it should so persistently produce books and lunacy?

On the outskirts of the forest, where shafts of dusty sunlight slanted through the trees, children were picking wortleberries for market as I passed last night, with hands and faces and aprons smudged into one blue stain. I had decided to go to a water-mill belonging to the Man of Wrath which lies far away in a clearing, so far away and so lonely and so quiet that the very spirit of peace seems to brood over it forever; and all the way the wortleberry carpet was thick and unbroken. Never were the pines more pungent than after the long heat, and their rosy stems flushed pinker as I passed. Presently I got beyond the region of wortleberry-pickers, the children not caring to wander too far into the forest so late, and I jolted over the roots into the gathering shadows more and more pervaded by that feeling that so refreshes me, the feeling of being absolutely alone.

A very ancient man lives in the mill and takes care of it, for it has long been unused, a deaf old man with a clean, toothless face, and no wife to worry him. He informed me once that all women are mistakes, especially that aggravated form called wives, and that he was thankful he had never married. I felt a certain delicacy after that about intruding on his solitude with the burden of my sex and wifehood heavy upon me, but he always seems very glad to see me, and runs at once to his fowlhouse to look for fresh eggs for my tea; so perhaps he regards me as a pleasing exception to the rule. On this last occasion he brought a table out to the elm-tree by the mill stream, that I might get what air there was while I ate my supper; and I sat in great peace waiting for the kettle to boil and watching the sun dropping behind the sharp forest me, and all the little pools and currents into which the stream just there breaks as it flows over mud banks, ablaze with the red reflection of the sky. The pools are clothed with water-lilies and inhabited by eels, and I generally take a netful of writhing eels back with me to the Man of Wrath to pacify him after my prolonged absence. In the lily time I get into the miller's punt and make them an excuse for paddling about among the mud islands, and even adventurously exploring the river as it winds into the forest, and the old man watches me anxiously from under the elm. He regards my feminine desire to pick water-lilies with indulgence, but is clearly uneasy at my affection for mud banks, and once, after I had stuck on one, and he had run up and down in great agitation for half an hour shouting instructions as to getting off again, he said when I was safely back on shore that people with petticoats (his way of expressing woman) were never intended for punts, and their only chance of safety lay in dry land and keeping quiet. I did not this time attempt the punt, for I was tired, and it was half full of water, probably poured into it by a miller weary of the ways of women; and I drank my tea quietly, going on at the same time with my interrupted afternoon reading of the *Sorrows of Werther*, in which I had reached a part that has a special fascination for me every time I read it—that part where

Werther first meets Lotte, and where, after a thunderstorm; they both go to the window, and she is so touched by the beauties of nature that she lays her hand on his and murmurs "Klopstock,"– to the complete dismay of the reader, though not of Werther, for he, we find, was so carried away by the magic word that he flung himself on to her hand and kissed it with tears of rapture.

I looked up from the book at the quiet pools and the black line of trees, above which stars were beginning to twinkle, my ears soothed by the splashing of the mill stream and the hooting somewhere near of a solitary owl, and I wondered whether, if the Man of Wrath were by my side, it would be a relief to my pleasurable feelings to murmur "Klopstock," and whether if I did he would immediately shed tears of joy over my hand. The name is an unfortunate one as far as music goes, and Goethe's putting it into his heroine's mouth just when she was most enraptured, seems to support the view I sometimes adopt in discoursing to the Man of Wrath that he had no sense of humour. But here I am talking about Goethe, our great genius and idol, in a way that no woman should. What do German women know of such things? Quite untrained and uneducated, how are we to judge rightly about anybody or anything? All we can do is to jump at conclusions, and, when we have jumped, receive with meekness the information that we have jumped wrong. Sitting there long after it was too dark to read, I thought of the old miller's words, and agreed with him that the best thing a woman can do in this world is to keep quiet. He came out once and asked whether he should bring a lamp, and seemed uneasy at my choosing to sit there in the dark. I could see the stars in the black pools, and a line of faint light far away above the pines where the sun had set. Every now and then the hot air from the ground struck up in my face, and afterwards would come a cooler breath from the water. Of what use is it to fight for things and make a noise? Nature is so clear in her teaching that he who has lived with her for any time can be in little doubt as to the "better way." Keep quiet and say one's prayers–certainly not merely the best, but the only things to do if one would be truly happy; but, ashamed of asking when I have received so much, the only form of prayer I would use would be a form of thanksgiving.

The Babies *in the* Buttercups

September

September 9th–I have been looking in the dictionary for the English word for *Einquartierung*, because that is what is happening to us just now, but I can find nothing satisfactory. My dictionary merely says (1) the quartering, (2) soldiers quartered, and then relapses into irrelevancy; so that it is obvious English people do without the word for the delightful reason that they have not got the thing. We have it here very badly; an epidemic raging at the end of nearly every summer, when cottages and farms swarm with soldiers and horses, when all the female part of the population gets engaged to be married and will not work, when all the male part is jealous and wants to fight, and when my house is crowded with individuals so brilliant and decorative in their dazzling uniforms that I wish sometimes I might keep a bunch of the tallest and slenderest forever in a big china vase in a corner of the drawing-room.

This year the manoeuvres are up our way, so that we are blest with more than our usual share of attention, and wherever you go you see soldiers, and the holy calm that has brooded over us all the summer has given place to a perpetual running to and fro of officers' servants, to meals being got ready at all hours, to the clanking of spurs and all those other mysterious things on an officer that do clank whenever he moves, and to the grievous wailings of my unfortunate menials, who are quite beside themselves, and know not whither to turn for succour. We have had one week of it already, and we have yet another before us. There are five hundred men with their horses quartered at the farm, and thirty officers with their servants in our house, besides all those billeted on the surrounding villages who have to be invited to dinner and cannot be allowed to perish in peasant houses; so that my summer has for a time entirely ceased to be solitary, and whenever I flee distracted to the farthest recesses of my garden and begin to muse, according to my habit, on Man, on Nature, and on Human Life, lieutenants got up in the most exquisite flannels pursue me and want to play tennis with me, a game I have always particularly disliked.

There is no room of course for all those extra men and horses at the farm, and when a few days before their arrival (sometimes it is only one, and sometimes only a few hours) an official appears and informs us of the number to be billeted on us, the Man of Wrath has to have temporary sheds run up, some as stables, some as sleeping-places, and some as dining-rooms. Nor is it easy to cook for five hundred people more than usual, and all the ordinary business of the farm comes to a stand-still while the hands prepare barrowfuls of bacon and potatoes, and stir up the coffee and milk and sugar together with a pole in a tub. Part of the regimental band is here, the upper part. The base instruments are in the next village; but that did not deter an enthusiastic young officer from marching his men past our windows on their arrival at six in the morning, with colours flying, and what he had of his band playing their tunes as unconcernedly as though all those big things that make such a noise were giving the fabric its accustomed and necessary base. We are paid six pfennings a day for lodging a common soldier, and six pfennings for his horse—rather more than a penny in English money for the pair of them; only unfortunately sheds and carpentry are not quite so cheap. Eighty pfennings a day is added for the soldier's food, and for this he has to receive two pounds of bread, half a pound of meat, a quarter of a pound of bacon, and either a quarter of a pound of rice or barley or three pounds of potatoes. Officers are paid for at the rate of two marks fifty a day without wine; we are not obliged to give them wine, and if we do they are regarded as guests, and behave accordingly. The thirty we have now do not, as I could have wished, all go out together in the morning and stay out till the evening, but some go out as others come in, and breakfast is not finished till lunch begins, and lunch drags on till dinner, and all day long the dining-room is full of meals and officers, and we ceased a week ago to have the least feeling that the place, after all, belongs to us.

Now really it seems to me that I am a much-tried woman, and any peace I have enjoyed up to now is amply compensated for by my present torments. I believe even my stern friend the missionary would be satisfied if he could know how swiftly his prediction that sorrow and suffering would be sure to come, has been fulfilled. All day long I am giving out table linen, ordering meals, supporting the feeble knees of servants, making appropriate and amiable remarks to officers, presiding as gracefully as nature permits at meals, and trying to look as though I were happy; while out in the garden—oh, I know how it is looking out in the garden this golden weather, how the placid hours are slipping by in unchanged peace, how strong the scent of roses and ripe fruit is, how the sleepy bees drone round the flowers, how warmly the sun shines in that corner where the little Spanish chestnut is turning yellow—the first to turn, and never afterwards surpassed in autumn beauty; I know how still it is down there in my fir wood, where the insects hum undisturbed in the warm, quiet air; I know what the plain looks like from the seat under the oak, how beautiful, with its rolling green waves burning to gold under the afternoon sky; I know how the hawks circle over it, and how the larks sing above it, and I edge as near to the open window as I can, straining my ears to hear them, and forgetting the young men who are telling me of all the races their horses win as completely as though they did not exist. I want to be out there on that golden grass, and look up into that endless blue, and feel the ecstasy of that song through all my being, and there is a tearing at my heart when I remember that I cannot. Yet they are beautiful young men; all are touchingly amiable, and many of the older ones even charming—how is it, then, that I so passionately prefer larks?

We have every grade of greatness here, from that innocent being the ensign, a creature of apparent modesty and blushes, who is obliged to stand up and drain his glass each time a superior chooses to drink to him, and who sits on the hardest chairs and looks for the balls while we play tennis, to the general, invariably delightful, whose brains have carried him triumphantly through the annual perils of weeding out, who is as distinguished in looks and manners as he is in abilities, and has the crowning merit of being manifestly happy in the society of women. Nothing lower than a colonel is to me an object of interest. The lower you get the more officers there are, and the harder it is to see the promising ones in the crowd; but once past the rank of major the air gets very much cleared by the merciless way they have been weeded out, and the higher officers are the very flower of middle-aged German males. As for those below, a lieutenant is a bright and beautiful being who admires no one so much as himself; a captain is generally newly married, having reached the stage of increased pay which makes a wife possible, and, being often still in love with her, is ineffective for social purposes; and a major is a man with a yearly increasing family, for whose wants his pay is inadequate, a person continually haunted by the fear of approaching weeding, after which his career is ended, he is poorer than ever, and being no longer young and only used to a soldier's life, is almost always quite incapable of starting afresh. Even the children of light find it difficult to start afresh with any success after forty, and the retired officer is never a child of light; if he were, he would not have been weeded out. You meet him everywhere, shorn of the glories of his uniform, easily recognisable by the bad fit of his civilian clothes, wandering about like a ship without a rudder; and as time goes on he settles down to the inevitable, and passes his days in a fourth-floor flat in the suburbs, eats, drinks, sleeps, reads the *Kreuzzeitung* and nothing else, plays at cards in the day-time, grows gouty, and worries his wife. It would be difficult to count the number of them that have answered the Man of Wrath's advertisements for book- keepers and secretaries—always vainly, for even if they were fit for the work, no single person possesses enough tact to cope successfully with the peculiarities of such a situation. I hear that some English people of a hopeful disposition indulge in ladies as servants; the cases are parallel, and the tact required to meet both superhuman.

Of all the officers here the only ones with whom I can find plenty to talk about are the generals. On what subject under heaven could one talk to a lieutenant? I cannot discuss the agility of ballet-dancers or the merits of jockeys with him, because these things are as dust and ashes to me; and when forced for a few moments by my duties as hostess to come within range of his conversation I feel chilly and grown old. In the early spring of this year, in those wonderful days of hope when nature is in a state of suppressed excitement, and when any day the yearly recurring miracle may happen of a few hours' warm rain changing the whole world, we got news that a lieutenant and two men with their horses were imminent, and would be quartered here for three nights while some occult military evolutions were going on a few miles off. It was specially inopportune, because the Man of Wrath would not be here, but he comforted me as I bade him good-bye, my face no doubt very blank, by the assurance that the lieutenant would be away all day, and so worn out when he got back in the evening that he probably would not appear at all. But I never met a more wide-awake young man. Not once during those three days did he respond to my pressing entreaties to go and lie down, and not all the desperate eloquence of a woman at her wit's end could persuade him that he was very tired and ought to try and get some sleep. I had intended to be out when he arrived, and to remain out till dinner time, but he came unexpectedly early, while the babies and I were still at lunch, the door opening to admit the most beautiful specimen of his class that I have ever seen, so beautiful indeed in his white uniform that the babies took him for an angel–visitant of the type that visited Abraham and Sarah, and began in whispers to argue about wings. He was not in the least tired after his long ride he told me, in reply to my anxious inquiries, and, rising to the occasion, at once plunged into conversation, evidently realising how peculiarly awful prolonged pauses under the circumstances would be. I took him for a drive in the afternoon, after having vainly urged him to rest, and while he told me about his horses, and his regiment, and his brother officers, in what at last grew to be a decidedly intermittent prattle, I amused myself by wondering what he would say if I suddenly began to hold forth on the themes I love best, and insist that he should note the beauty of the trees as they stood that afternoon expectant, with all their little buds only waiting for the one warm shower to burst into the glory of young summer. Perhaps he would regard me as the German variety of a hyena in petticoats—the imagination recoils before the probable fearfulness of such an animal—or, if not quite so bad as that, at any rate a creature hysterically inclined; and he would begin to feel lonely, and think of his comrades, and his pleasant mess, and perhaps even of his mother, for he was very young and newly fledged. Therefore I held my peace, and restricted my conversation to things military, of which I know probably less than any other woman in Germany, so that my remarks must have been to an unusual degree impressive. He talked down to me, and I talked down to him, and we reached home in a state of profoundest exhaustion—at least I know I did, but when I looked at him he had not visibly turned a hair. I went upstairs trying to hope that he had felt it more than he showed, and that during the remainder of his stay he would adopt the suggestion so eagerly offered of spending his spare time in his room resting.

At dinner, he and I, quite by ourselves, were both manifestly convinced of the necessity, for the sake of the servants, of not letting the conversation drop. I felt desperate, and would have said anything sooner than sit opposite him in silence, and with united efforts we got through that fairly well. After dinner I tried gossip, and encouraged him to tell me some, but he had such an unnatural number of relations that whoever I began to talk about happened to be his cousin, or his brother- in-law, or his aunt, as he hastily informed me, so that what I had intended to say had to be turned immediately into loud and unqualified praise; and praising people is frightfully hard work—you give yourself the greatest pains over it, and are aware all the time that it is not in the very least carrying conviction. Does not everybody know that one's natural impulse is to tear the absent limb from limb? At half-past nine I got up, worn out in mind and body, and told him very firmly that it had been a custom in my family from time immemorial to be in bed by ten, and that I was accordingly going there. He looked surprised and wider awake than ever, but nothing shook me, and I walked away, leaving him standing on the hearthrug after the manner of my countrymen, who never dream of opening a door for a woman.

The next day he went off at five in the morning, and was to be away, as he had told me, till the evening. I felt as though I had been let out of prison as I breakfasted joyfully on the verandah, the sun streaming through the creeperless trellis on to the little meal, and the first cuckoo of the year calling to me from the fir wood. Of the dinner and evening before me I would not think; indeed I had a half-formed plan in my head of going to the forest after lunch with the babies, taking wraps and provisions, and getting lost till well on towards bedtime; so that when the angel-visitant should return full of renewed strength and conversation, he would find the casket empty and be told the gem had gone out for a walk. After I had finished breakfast I ran down the steps into the garden, intent on making the most of every minute and hardly able to keep my feet from dancing. Oh, the blessedness of a bright spring morning without a lieutenant! And was there ever such a hopeful beginning to a day, and so full of promise for the subsequent right passing of its hours, as breakfast in the garden, alone with your teapot and your book! Any cobwebs that have clung to your soul from the day before are brushed off with a neatness and expedition altogether surprising; never do tea and toast taste so nice as out there in the sun; never was a book so wise and full of pith as the one lying open before you; never was woman so clean outside and in, so refreshed, so morally and physically well-tubbed, as she who can start her day in this fashion. As I danced down the garden path I began to think cheerfully even of lieutenants. It was not so bad; he would be away till dark, and probably on the morrow as well; I would start off in the afternoon, and by coming back very late would not see him at all that day–might not, if Providence were kind, see him again ever; and this last thought was so exhilarating that I began to sing. But he came back just as we had finished lunch.

"The *Herr Lieutenant* is here," announced the servant, "and has gone to wash his hands. The *Herr Lieutenant* has not yet lunched, and will be down in a moment."

"I want the carriage at once," I ordered–I could not and would not spend another afternoon *tete-a-tete* with that young man,–"and you are to tell the *Herr Lieutenant* that I am sorry I was obliged to go out, but I had promised the pastor to take the children there this afternoon. See that he has everything he wants."

I gathered the babies together and fled. I could hear the lieutenant throwing things about overhead, and felt there was not a moment to lose. The servant's face showed plainly that he did not believe about the pastor, and the babies looked up at me wonderingly. What is a woman to do when driven into a corner? The father of lies inhabits corners—no doubt the proper place for such a naughty person.

We ran upstairs to get ready. There was only one short flight on which we could meet the lieutenant, and once past that we were safe; but we met him on that one short flight. He was coming down in a hurry, giving his moustache a final hasty twist, and looking fresher, brighter, lovelier, than ever.

"Oh, good morning. You have got back much sooner than you expected, have you not?" I said lamely.

"Yes, I managed to get through my part quickly," he said with a briskness I did not like.

"But you started so early—you must be very tired?"

"Oh, not in the least, thank you."

Then I repeated the story about the expectant parson, adding to my guilt by laying stress on the inevitability of the expedition owing to its having been planned weeks before. April and May stood on the landing above, listening with surprised faces, and June, her mind evidently dwelling on feathers, intently examined his shoulders from the step immediately behind. And we did get away, leaving him to think what he liked, and to smoke, or sleep, or wander as he chose, and I could not but believe he must feel relieved to be rid of me; but the afternoon clouded over, and a sharp wind sprang up, and we were very cold in the forest, and the babies began to sneeze and ask where the parson was, and at last, after driving many miles, I said it was too late to go to the parson's and we would turn back. It struck me as hard that we should be forced to wander in cold forests and leave our comfortable home because of a lieutenant, and I went back with my heart hardened against him.

That second evening was worse a great deal than the first. We had said all we ever meant to say to each other, and had lauded all our relations with such hearty goodwill that there was nothing whatever to add. I sat listening to the slow ticking of the clock and asking questions about things I did not in the least want to know, such as the daily work and rations and pay of the soldiers in his regiment, and presently–we having dined at the early hour usual in the country–the clock struck eight. Could I go to bed at eight? No, I had not the courage, and no excuse ready. More slow ticking, and more questions and answers about rations and pipeclay. What a clock! For utter laziness and dull deliberation there surely never was its equal–it took longer to get to the half-hour than any clock I ever met, but it did get there at last and struck it. Could I go? Could I? No, still no excuse ready. We drifted from pipeclay to a discussion on bicycling for women–a dreary subject. Was it becoming? Was it good for them? Was it ladylike? Ought they to wear skirts or–? In Paris they all wore–. Our bringing-up here is so excellent that if we tried we could not induce ourselves to speak of any forked garments to a young man, so we make ourselves understood, when we desire to insinuate such things, by an expressive pause and a modest downward flicker of the eyelids. The clock struck nine. Nothing should keep me longer. I sprang to my feet and said I was exhausted beyond measure by the sharp air driving, and that whenever I had spent an afternoon out, it was my habit to go to bed half an hour earlier than other evenings. Again he looked surprised, but rather less so than the night before, and he was, I think, beginning to get used to me. I retired, firmly determined not to face another such day and to be very ill in the morning and quite unable to rise, he having casually remarked that the next one was an off day; and I would remain in bed, that last refuge of the wretched, as long as he remained here.

I sat by the window in my room till late, looking out at the moonlight in the quiet garden, with a feeling as though I were stuffed with sawdust–a very awful feeling–and thinking ruefully of the day that had begun so brightly and ended so dismally. What a miserable thing not to be able to be frank and say simply, "My good young man, you and I never saw each other before, probably won't see each other again, and have no interests in common. I mean you to be comfortable in my house, but I want to be comfortable too. Let us, therefore, keep out of each other's way while you are obliged to be here. Do as you like, go where you like, and order what you like, but don't expect me to waste my time sitting by your side and making small-talk. I too have to get to heaven, and have no time to lose. You won't see me again. Good-bye."

I believe many a harassed *Hausfrau* would give much to be able to make some such speech when these young men appear, and surely the young men themselves would be grateful; but simplicity is apparently quite beyond people's strength. It is, of all the virtues, the one I prize the most; it is undoubtedly the most lovable of any, and unspeakably precious for its power of removing those mountains that confine our lives and prevent our seeing the sky. Certain it is that until we have it, the simple spirit of the little child, we shall in no wise discover our kingdom of heaven.

These were my reflections, and many others besides, as I sat weary at the window that cold spring night, long after the lieutenant who had occasioned them was slumbering peacefully on the other side of the house. Thoughts of the next day, and enforced bed, and the bowls of gruel to be disposed of if the servants were to believe in my illness, made my head ache. Eating gruel *pour la galerie* is a pitiable state to be reduced to—surely no lower depths of humiliation are conceivable. And then, just as I was drearily remembering how little I loved gruel, there was a sudden sound of wheels rolling swiftly round the corner of the house, a great rattling and trampling in the still night over the stones, and tearing open the window and leaning out, there, sitting in a station fly, and apparelled to my glad vision in celestial light, I beheld the Man of Wrath, come home unexpectedly to save me.

"Oh, dear Man of Wrath," I cried, hanging out into the moonlight with outstretched arms, "how much nicer thou art than lieutenants! I never missed thee more—I never longed for thee more—I never loved thee more —come up here quickly that I may kiss thee!—"

October 1st.–Last night after dinner, when we were in the library, I said, "Now listen to me, Man of Wrath."

"Well?" he inquired, looking up at me from the depths of his chair as I stood before him.

"Do you know that as a prophet you are a failure? Five months ago to-day you sat among the wallflowers and scoffed at the idea of my being able to enjoy myself alone a whole summer through. Is the summer over?"

"It is," he assented, as he heard the rain beating against the windows.

"And have I invited any one here?"

"No, but there were all those officers."

"They have nothing whatever to do with it."

"They helped you through one fortnight."

"They didn't. It was a fortnight of horror."

"Well. Go on."

"You said I would be punished by being dull. Have I been dull?"

"My dear, as though if you had been you would ever confess it."

"That's true. But as a matter of fact let me tell you that I never spent a happier summer."

He merely looked at me out of the corners of his eyes.

"If I remember rightly," he said, after a pause, "your chief reason for wishing to be solitary was that your soul might have time to grow. May I ask if it did?"

"Not a bit."

He laughed, and, getting up, came and stood by my side before the fire. "At least you are honest," he said, drawing my hand through his arm.

"It is an estimable virtue."

"And strangely rare in woman."

"Now leave woman alone. I have discovered you know nothing really of her at all. But *I* know all about her."

"You do? My dear, one woman can never judge the others."

"An exploded tradition, dear Sage."

"Her opinions are necessarily biassed."

"Venerable nonsense, dear Sage."

"Because women are each other's natural enemies."

"Obsolete jargon, dear Sage."

"Well, what do you make of her?"

"Why, that she's a DEAR, and that you ought to be very happy and thankful to have got one of her always with you."

"But am I not?" he asked, putting his arm round me and looking affectionate; and when people begin to look affectionate I, for one, cease to take any further interest in them.

And so the Man of Wrath and I fade away into dimness and muteness, my head resting on his shoulder, and his arm encircling my waist; and what could possibly be more proper, more praiseworthy, or more picturesque?

The End

CPSIA information can be obtained at www.ICGtesting.com
Printed in the USA
LVOW060054230513

335076LV00002B/351/P